What people are saying about the *Simplified Strategic Planning* process...

Using Simplified Strategic Planning, *VPI tripled sales over five years. It has helped us identify opportunities, better understand our markets, and focus our resources to attain the business results we desired. It has contributed in a significant way to VPI achieving our growth and profit objectives.*

> T. Godfrey Mackenzie, Vice President
> Vinyl Plastics, Inc.

What we accomplished during our seven days of work was unprecedented in our company's history. We have defined a consensus among the top management as to what kind of a company we will be for the next five years. Establishing this shared vision and the means to achieve it would not have been possible without strategic planning. This process is extremely well organized and compelling, while allowing the special human attributes of our organization to flourish.

> Harris C. Footer, President and CEO
> Easy Day Manufacturing Company

The Simplified Strategic Planning *process is a perfect fit for a company our size. It provides a solid theoretical approach that is applied in a very real world down-to-earth manner. The program does an excellent job of providing a defined framework for the planning process without turning it into a mechanistic "fill out the form" exercise. The framework helped us make sure that we were identifying and analyzing the key issues; it did not do our thinking for us. Finally, I feel the emphasis on the development of specific objectives and action plans is the key to ensuring that strategic planning isn't just an interesting annual exercise that subsequently collects dust on a bookshelf. I know the strategic plan we produced will make a major difference in the performance of our business.*

> Roger A. Carolin, President and CEO
> CFM Technologies, Inc.

It is difficult for managers in small- or medium-sized operations to escape the day-to-day hectic pace, since we are generally in the thick of operations and not insulated by support staffs. The approach presented in Simplified Strategic Planning *is very pragmatic, and should enable an organization such as ours to address the critical components of strategic planning, while avoiding wasted effort in the plan "filler" that often accompanies such efforts. This process places a priority on closure in the strategic decision-making process and facilitates follow-up to help ensure that the planning effort is not a wasted annual exercise with no closure.*

> Frank G. Edwards, CFO
> Carl M. Freeman Associates, Inc.

... A great tool for acheiving strategic alignment and keeping "the main thing the main thing."

> Veronne Williams, Sr. VP
> Innovative Logistics Techniques, Inc.

Simplified Strategic Planning *provided us a straightforward process that helped our already successful organization set a much clearer direction for the future.*

> Jack Lowe, Jr., CEO
> TD Industries
> (#2 of *Fortune* 100 Best Companies
> to Work for in America)

Simplified Strategic Planning

**A No-Nonsense Guide for Busy
People Who Want Results Fast!**

Simplified
Strategic Planning

A No-Nonsense Guide for Busy People Who Want Results Fast!

**Robert W. Bradford
and J. Peter Duncan**
With Brian Tarcy

**Chandler House Press
Worcester, Massachusetts**

Simplified Strategic Planning:
A No-Nonsense Guide for Busy People Who Want Results Fast!

ISBN 1-886284-46-6
Library of Congress Catalog Card Number: 99-65619
First Edition
        JK

Published by
Chandler House Press
335 Chandler Street
Worcester, MA 01602 USA

President
Lawrence J. Abramoff

Book Design and Production
John Woods, CWL Publishing Enterprises
www.cwlpub.com

Cover Design
Marshall Henrichs

Cover Photo
Larry Williams - Masterfile

Chandler House Press specializes in custom publishing for businesses, organizations, and individuals. For more information on how to publish through our corporation, please contact Chandler House Press, 335 Chandler Street, Worcester, MA 01602. Call (800) 642-6657, fax (508) 756-9425, or find us on the World Wide Web at www.chandlerhousepress.com.

Contents

Foreword

ROBERT BRADFORD AND PETER DUNCAN HAVE WRITTEN a breakthrough book on strategy. Throughout my 25-year career as a business school professor, first at Columbia University and then at the University of Michigan, and as a practitioner, including my stint in the 1980s heading up GE's world renowned leadership development center, Crotonville, I have wrestled with teaching and coaching MBA students and executives around strategy. What makes *Simplified Strategic Planning* such a breakthrough is that it provides the intellectual and practical guidance for business leaders to get on with the task of setting a winning strategy.

In the book on my GE experiences, *Control Your Destiny or Someone Else Will: How Jack Welch Is Making General Electric the World's Most Competitive Enterprise*, Jack Welch states, "I chose one of the simpler professions in life, business, it is not rocket science regarding what people do, execution is the name of the game." He also points out that strategy follows people. In *Simplified Strategic Planning*, Peter and Robert drive the same point: get the people dimension right, keep strategy simple, and execute for results.

Simplified Strategic Planning presents a straightforward, no-nonsense formula for developing winning strategies that get successfully executed. The process is not rocket science, but that is the genius. As Jack Welch points out, it takes self-confident leaders to be simple, which is what gives them focus and speed in the market place. By reading *Simplified Strategic Planning*, each of you will be able to develop your own framework set of guiding principles for leading strategy.

This book will teach you how to develop your own approach to strategic planning, one that captures the spirit of what Welch so clearly embodies in his leadership. Drawing on over 30 years of experience coaching and mentoring business leaders, Peter Duncan and Robert Bradford have written an invaluable guide to your success as a business leader. *Simplified Strategic Planning* provides you with a template and practical tools for ensuring a winning strategy and a process that can continuously reinvent your organization for tomorrow's competitive landscape.

Noel Tichy
University of Michigan
Ann Arbor, MI

Preface

How do you picture success? Would you like to double your operating margins and double your sales volume within three years? Would that be success? Or how about a way to improve accountability so that you get at least 90% of your key projects done each year? What kind of results would that bring you?

Could you get excited about executing a profitable new opportunity that within a year quadruples your annual revenue—$5 million in sales goes to $20 million? What about leading a company to the very top of the "*Fortune 100 Best Companies to Work for in America*" list? Do you picture yourself creating great enterprise?

Great enterprise is the stuff of dreams and hard work, yet success takes something more. Great results do not happen by accident. Instead, successful companies use detailed and flexible plans to plot their course and direction. But those plans don't have to be complicated.

Simplified Strategic Planning offers a roadmap to your dreams—a roadmap that along the way answers the essential questions of business:

- What are you going to sell?
- Who are your target customers?
- How can you beat or avoid the competition?

With strategy, you get to choose, but those choices do not have to be complicated. With a time-proven method for putting together a strategic plan, *Simplified Strategic Planning* takes you on a step-by-step journey. As you learn to identify an appropriate course and direction for your company or organization, you will encounter telling examples of how companies have followed this process and dramatically improved their results. This process is detailed, but it is not complicated.

Step by step, this book teaches what to study in the internal and external environments, as well as how to make assumptions about the future.

Simplified Strategic Planning is more than philosophy, more than a fad or flavor of the month. This book brings a refreshing break from the pop solutions and management buzzwords that have permeated business publishing over the past decade. Instead of another one-dimensional panacea, *Simplified Strategic Planning* draws together some of the most insightful business thinking of the past 25 years in a simple, doable process that any manager can use to achieve great results in an organization.

As you read you will learn:

- To take control of your destiny by establishing a lean, effective strategy process.
- To develop an ongoing program to assess and understand your business environment.
- To develop appropriate and insightful assumptions about the future.
- To assess and make strategic choices in order to develop a clear achievable focus.
- To translate the company vision into personal involvement for key employees.
- To monitor results and continually adapt to changing conditions.

And in the course of completing the exercises dispersed throughout the chapters, readers will actually develop a strategic plan for their business. *Simplified Strategic Planning* offers something most business books can only dream of offering—it offers a way to do it.

How to Use This Book

Think of this as a cookbook—a "how to" manual that you work through as you read along. Of course, you may read it cover to cover, and then come back and do the work, but be sure to do the work. Reading alone will not bring the same value as actually using this process.

This book is packed with tips, techniques, and tools to help you emerge from the last chapter with a strategic plan in hand. You'll find four types of sidebars that provide examples and instructions for moving through your planning process:

- **Tales from the Strategy Vault**. Stories that illustrate the text.
- **Strategic Tip**. Hints, suggestions, or concepts for better strategic thinking.
- **In the Meeting**. Things you should do with your team in one of the three scheduled meetings.
- **Outside the Meeting**. Assignments or preparation you should do before a scheduled meeting.

Use of Worksheets

Where there is specific information you need to develop as part of the process, we have included worksheets. Computer templates are available for downloading on our Web site, www.simplifiedstrategy.com. These should be completed as you work through the book. They will become your strategic plan. As you go through the process, put these into a loose-leaf notebook for team members to use during both planning and implementation.

Figure Numbers and Page Numbers on Worksheets

In the simplified strategic planning process, we use a series of worksheets to help people collect information and move through the process. These worksheets, filled in with the kind of information they call for, appear as figures throughout this book. Each worksheet has a worksheet number in the upper right corner that indicates how it should be sequenced in your loose-leaf notebook. The appendix at the end of this book has a list of these worksheets, the order in which they should appear in a loose-leaf planning notebook, and the pages in this book where you can find examples of how they should be filled out.

The Case

The example worksheets in this book are illustrated with a case study. We have chosen a simple company—a small packaging company that makes boxes for the candy and bakery industry. These boxes have interior components (layer cards, dividers, etc.) to protect the contents and decorative exterior boxes to promote the contents. The boxes are used to package various types of candy and bakery goods for commercial and retail sale.

We have chosen this simple example to make it easy to see the elements of a good simplified strategic plan without being distracted by the complexity of the example. We selected a manufacturing company because it's often easier to describe and relate to a physical product. This process is frequently used with companies that are more complex than our small packaging company and it is just as suitable for service organizations and non-manufacturing companies.

How This Book Is Organized

The text is divided into five parts that follow the process you should go through in developing a strategic plan.

Part 1, Embrace the Top Priority of Management, addresses the conceptual underpinnings of planning, the all-important elements of team formation and leadership, and provides an overview of the simplified strategic planning process.

Part 2, Start by Studying the Way It Is Now, answers the question, "Where are we?" The information developed in this section forms an important reference point for the planning process. Here we determine our markets, identify competitors, and study the overall climate for our business.

Part 3, Figure Out the Way You Expect Things to Be, deals with your assumptions about the future. Assumptions are a critical part of the planning process. They must be explicit and agreed to before decisions can be made. In this section you develop assumptions about your markets, competitors, business environment, opportunities, threats, and the long-term trends in your industry.

Part 4, Design Your Future, answers the question, "Where do we want to go?" Here you pull together all of the analysis and shift into making the decisions and choices that become your strategy. That vision for the organization is captured in a simple outline. This section concludes with making commitments to your strategy—commitments that will lead to tangible results for your business.

Part 5, Create a Way to Get Things Done, addresses questions of implementing your strategy: "How will we get there?" "Who is responsible?" "How much will it cost?" "When will we arrive?" Action plans, budgets, and personal time plans put teeth into the process and lead you to what you want—real results that will optimize the potential of your business.

How Are You Doing?

Thanks for buying this book. It seems only fair that part of what you get with a book is the opportunity to talk to the authors, so here's your chance. We'll try to reply quickly. You can reach us via e-mail at the addresses below:

Robert Bradford: rbradford@simplifiedstrategy.com
Peter Duncan: duncan@simplifiedstrategy.com

We like to be in contact with those who are using *Simplified Strategic Planning*, so let us know how you are doing. We really welcome questions and suggestions—that's the way we improve our stuff. Drop us a line and let us know how this process is working for you.

The Center for Simplified Strategic Planning has always maintained an "open door" policy. We are committed to providing the best thinking in strategic planning for smaller and mid-size organizations. This book is just one way to do that. Another is our Web site—www.simplifiedstrategy.com. It's loaded with other information. Visit us now to introduce yourself, then come back later to keep up to date on the latest in strategic planning.

Or you can contact us by mail at
The Center for Simplified Strategic Planning, Inc.
P.O. Box 851
Southport, CT 06490-0851

Trademarks

All terms that are or are thought to be trademarks, service marks, or other legally protected materials referenced in this work have been appropriately capitalized and are the property of their rightful owners. Inclusion in this work should not be regarded as having any effect on the validity or ownership of any trademarks or service marks.

Acknowledgments

WE WOULD LIKE TO THANK SOME PEOPLE who helped us bring this project from dreams to publication. First, we want to thank Larry Abramoff, President of Chandler House Press and the full editorial team at Chandler House who have made this book possible. We also would like to thank Michael Snell of the Michael Snell Literary Agency for his guidance in helping us sell the idea. And we thank Richard Staron for recognizing the value of *Simplified Strategic Planning* and launching this project.

Betty Shaughnessy of the Atlantic Edtek Typing was fast and accurate with transcriptions of our conversations, and Jennifer Goguen, editorial/production manager at Chandler House Press, proved heroic in bringing this project through its final steps. John Woods and Robert Magnan of CWL Publishing Enterprises transformed this manuscript into the book you now hold. We also want to thank our publicist, Claire Cousineau Smith, and Noel Tichy of the University of Michigan for writing the foreword to this work. Suzanne Simmonds, Tina Granzo, and Paul Moorehead who did the graphic design on some of the early drafts of this work and got us to the next stage.

We also offer appreciation to our colleagues—Tom Ambler, Dana Baldwin, Denise Harrison, Paul Minton, Steve Rutan, and Barry Wolfson—and clients who have enriched this book with insights and examples.

The authors also thank Chuck Bradford for his foresight, teaching, and inspiration. Always at the forefront of critical thinking, Chuck was years ahead of others when he developed Simplified Strategic Planning. He put the process together and, with patience, he taught the process and inspired us to build on his foundation and develop this work. Chuck, your support for each of us and this book has been essential to its success.

Robert Bradford. I would like to thank Jeannette Jackson, who not only gave me support and much needed critiques, but also sacrificed a great deal to let me sleep when I most needed it. Also, I owe much to Maria Coolican for her encouragement and helpful suggestions. My wonderful children, Madeleine and John, encouraged me as only they can.

It goes without saying that Brian and Peter deserve a lot of thanks from me as well, not just for their fine contributions to the book itself, but for undertaking the difficult task of helping me keep my nose to the grindstone despite a plethora of enticing distractions. Their job was made much easier by the diligent work of Tina Granzo and Suzanne Simmonds.

I learned much of what I know about strategic thinking from Brian Quinn and John Shank of the Amos Tuck School, as well as Michael Hay of the London Business School. All three are superb teachers, a fact which is too often overlooked in the world of academia.

Finally, it should be noted that this book would not exist without the pioneering work of my father, Charles Bradford. He invented Simplified Strategic Planning and did the most difficult early trial-and-error testing of many of the concepts that we at the Center for Simplified Strategic Planning use every day in our work.

Peter Duncan. I would like to thank my co-authors Brian Tarcy and Robert Bradford. Brian, you made this book possible by keeping us on track, asking the tough questions, and making sure we explained things so that anyone could understand. Throughout, you have been tireless and persistent. Always upbeat, it has been fun to work with you. You have been much more than a writer; you have become a friend and colleague.

Robert, as always, your bold style and creativity has been an essential ingredient for this book. Who would have thought that running the social committee and night ski racing at Tuck would have led to the fun of working together and the satisfaction of this project. Thanks for bringing me to the Center for Simplified Strategic Planning.

I would also like to thank Chuck Bradford for the opportunity to work at the center. You are a great coach and mentor, and have built a terrific company that challenges me to do my best.

My profound appreciation goes out to all who have shaped my formal and informal education: my clients—I've learned a lot from you; my colleagues in business at the center and in the semiconductor industry; and my teachers and professors at Landon, Middlebury, and Tuck. I give special thanks to Professors James Brian Quinn and Vijay Govindarajan of the Amos Tuck School at Dartmouth—you taught me the fundamentals of business strategy that appear in this book.

To my colleagues at the center, Paul Minton and Barry Wolfson, you offered support and urged this project onward even when it seemed hopelessly stalled. And to Suzanne Simmonds, thank you for taking care of more details than I can count, with unflappable grace.

I offer a special thank you to my parents, John and Carol Duncan: you have always believed in me and inspired me to strive to make a difference in the world. And I thank my aunt, Alice Duncan, for your support of my career development.

In conclusion, I offer my heartfelt thanks my family. To my children, Ian, Terry, and Stephen: you have been most patient with my year-long obsession with "the book," but our play breaks have been the right medicine to keep me sane. And finally to my wife Sylvi: you inspire me and bring out the best in me. Your tireless efforts make this career possible for me. Thank you for all of the love, support, and many cups of hot tea that have gone into this project.

Brian Tarcy. I would first like to thank Robert Bradford and Peter Duncan for your professionalism, guidance and patience as I learned the process of Simplified Strategic Planning. I felt like I earned my MBA doing this book, and you were my professors. Thanks for the education and your friendship. You showed me the truth—this stuff really works.

I would also like to thank Gary Sutton and, especially, Hap Klopp, for giving me a foundation in the world of business. Your patience with my lack of business knowledge was legendary. It would've been easy to give up on me but you never did, and there are good books out there because you didn't.

I want to thank my parents, Paul and Dorothy Tarcy, and my brothers, Gary and Dave, for teaching me that knowledge is good. I want to thank Paul Sigler, Vaughn Sterling, Paul and Heidi Perekrests, Martha and Seneca Anderson, and Gregg Alexander for sticking with me a few years back when it seemed no one else would. I will never forget your kindness. And I want to thank Miles, Morgan, and Tristan Anders, and Jason Rutledge for simply being cool people.

Professionally, I want to thank Dick Staron and Mike Snell for allowing me the opportunity to learn stuff like this. It's fun to learn, and I learned a ton.

I want to thank my best friend, Maureen Anders, for putting up with this crazy career of mine. You become more precious to me every moment. Finally, I want to thank my children, Denim, Derek, Kayli, and Marissa—because of you I know I am the richest man on earth.

Part One

Embrace the Top Priority of Management

EVERY DAY IN YOUR LIFE AND IN YOUR WORK, THE CHOICE IS YOURS: you can drift or you can set out to accomplish something great. If you want to accomplish something great, you have to make a decision. What exactly do you want to accomplish?

In this first part, you'll learn that setting a course and direction must be the top priority of management. We'll start by addressing the concept of plotting your future while we explain the process flow for developing strategy—which is really a vision painted dot by dot. We'll discuss the makeup of a good strategic planning team. Then we'll address the three key questions of strategy:

- What are you going to sell?
- Who are your target customers?
- How can you beat or avoid the competition?

The undertaking is great, but the approach is simple and straightforward. The top priority of management is to ensure that there's a shared vision for the future of the organization and that this vision is a part of the culture.

So we ask, "What is your destination? What future do you seek?" It's time to take the first step toward your answer.

chapter 1

Strategic Planning: See a Future

I S YOUR COMPANY MOVING IN THE RIGHT DIRECTION? Are you moving in the right direction—as an individual, as an employee, as a leader? And just what is the right direction anyway?

Every business has a course and direction, just like a sailboat on the ocean. Left alone, the boat drifts with the wind and currents. But if a captain and officers have a destination in mind and take control of the boat, it becomes a vehicle to get to the future, a vehicle for realizing dreams.

But many sound companies with smart managers struggle to realize their dreams. As we have traveled the country for the past 15 years giving seminars, we and others at The Center for Simplified Strategic Planning (CSSP) have heard of many challenges that might sound familiar to you:

- I've reengineered the company but we still can't seem to make money. I've cut costs to the bone but the competition keeps eating us up.
- Our customers keep pressuring us. They expect us to exceed their expectations, give them outstanding service *and* low price—how can anyone make money at that game?
- We've blasted the traditional organizational structure, empowered the workers, and built teams. We have a different organization but the same old performance.

3

- The last two years we have had strong revenue growth, but falling profits. Strategy isn't the problem—it's finding the time to execute strategy at a small company like ours. We already have full-time jobs.
- We put in the best quality systems that money can buy. We are state-of-the-art and might even make a run at a Baldrige award, but our customers don't seem to appreciate our efforts. They expect quality and demand more in other areas, like delivery and lower price.
- We are a small player in an industry dominated by giants—and the big just keep getting bigger. We can't match their resources, so how can we compete? How can we survive?
- I've gone to every management seminar on every topic. We've tried them all. We get short bursts of improvement, but soon slip back to mediocre performance.

Each story is a little different, but many have a common thread. For many managers, today's popular business advice has become an ocean of panaceas for all corporate ills. And managers are drowning as they wonder, When the flavor of the week doesn't taste quite as good after about a week, then what?

Then you get back to the fundamentals—strategy is not some gimmick or fad or flavor of the week. According to research by Bain & Company (*Fortune*, September 7, 1998), strategy is the No. 1 tool companies use to gain advantage.

The future should not be a vague concept and strategy should not be a monstrous task in which we take pride in complexity. Strategy can be simple. Yes, it must be comprehensive, but it doesn't have to be complicated. And it's important—as important to companies as the building blocks of talent, drive, and resources in determining the ultimate success of a company.

> ### Tales from the Strategy Vault
>
> The Malcolm Baldrige Award is given annually to companies that have extremely high quality. In 1990 the Wallace Company, a family-run distributor of pipes and valves in Houston, won in the small business category. This company was the darling of those out to prove that excellent quality systems can be the salvation for any business. Unfortunately, glowing reviews didn't transfer into results: quality alone wasn't the recipe for success, not for this firm. The award did nothing to overcome a severe downturn in the oil business and a loss of focus by the management team. A few years later the company was in bankruptcy.

We all experience the present. Unfortunately, too few of us really plan for the future. You can revel, marvel, or wallow in your present existence.

But no matter how good or bad it is, it's going to change. A good strategy will help you anticipate and focus on possibilities—learning that it's as important to eliminate choices as to pursue them.

The future is coming, whether you're ready or not. If you're ready to meet it, you will succeed in business, in life, in anything. But being ready to meet the future means more than simply jutting out your jaw with the courage of a soldier. You need the plans of a general.

Strategy is about seeing the options and making the choices. That's what a general does—every time that the situation changes significantly.

Why Bother to Plan?

Managers need to understand that business is a very fluid thing. Whatever the business, it's going to change, and the pace is quickening (Figure 1-1). Whatever the circumstance, it will change. In fact, change is not just happening, but at a rapidly accelerating pace, and Darwinian principles will select the survivors. Organizations that try to resist change will fail to adapt and will then lose out. Change is inevitable; if you can't adapt, you won't survive. History makes this clear: standing still means death.

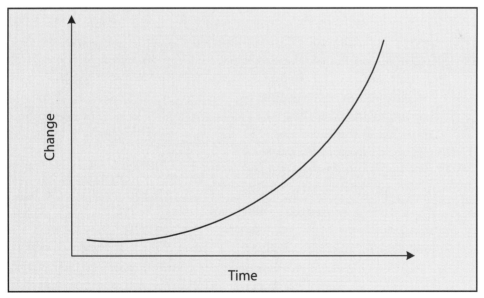

Figure 1-1. The pace of change is always increasing

Yesterday's Gone

Maybe you have been successful, maybe even wildly successful. Well, great! Allow yourself a moment of congratulations—but then recognize that it doesn't matter anymore. What matters now is what's going to happen in the coming years. What's next?

Time Marches On

- At the end of World War I, the Maginot Line was created under the assumption that the next war would be fought in the trenches by armies charging against each other. But the next war, World War II, turned out to be a very different war, with blitzkriegs, fast tanks, and airplanes. Wars continually prove this basic point: you can't craft the future by looking backwards.
- From before the turn of the century until the 1940s, Baldwin Locomotive Works was one of the largest companies in the country. The company manufactured steam engines for locomotives. But in the 1930s and 1940s, the company ran into a major technological challenge as the locomotive industry began moving away from coal-burning steam engines and toward electric and diesel motors. Baldwin made a crucial error. At a time when the two "generals"—General Electric and General Motors—dominated electric and diesel motors, Baldwin Locomotive Works decided to compete with those two giants on their turf. Baldwin shifted its top people into the new areas of diesel and electric motors. But Baldwin was too late and trying to dominate the wrong industry. The managers thought it was a transportation company but it was really a company that specialized in steam engines. They learned the truth the hard way.
- For a long time utility companies have been an example of businesses that were relatively immune to change. Their strategy was dominated by regulation and "rate of return" economics. Today, everything has changed. Electric companies deliver natural gas, water, and cable TV, while cable TV competes with your local phone company. The telephone, a network designed for five-minute voice calls, has become our access to the Internet, with "off-hook" times commonly reaching several hours and unlimited long-distance calls for the price of flat-rate local service.

What will tomorrow bring? Those who fail to figure this out will rapidly fall behind, while those who can get a bead on it will have the inside track to success.

Today Is Yesterday's Future

You got here somehow. Although your job in strategic planning is to consider what's next, a firm grasp of the past is important as a foundation for planning your future. So we begin with questions about the past.

What is the historical performance of your markets? Are they growing or shrinking? What is your financial performance—profitable or unprofitable? What have your competitors been doing? What are the trends in technology?

A certain sequence of choices brought you to this point. Although extrapolation is not easy in every business, it's still instructive to consider recent events and outcomes. What led to those? Nothing is guaranteed in business, but the results of an activity often establish a pattern that may be worth considering again. So, what just happened and how did you get here?

The past is full of road signs. Figuring out what has happened up to now is not rocket science, but it takes some research and work. A lot of people don't bother to do it; that's a mistake because you need that point of reference. Just as you cannot successfully drive a car by looking only in the rearview mirror, history cannot tell you where you are going. But it can tell you how you got here and it can give you clues to the road ahead. Remember: back then, this was the future.

Complexity Lives

It is common for would-be gurus to promote some single idea to make things great. Everybody wants the silver bullet and there are plenty of consultants, authors, and advisors out there promoting their latest cure for all business ills. There's always something new, a different flavor each month: Total Quality Management, Reengineering, Guerrilla Marketing, Change Leadership .... The list goes on and on. Just check out the names of all the books that are offering a single panacea. Some of it works, at least somewhat. But it's a rare concept that's powerful enough to solve all problems. If the world were that simplistic, somebody would have figured it out a long time ago.

You cannot usually solve a complex problem with a one-dimensional approach. Business is complex and it can be frustrating when the single solution doesn't really work. Instead, you need a big-picture, balanced approach to look at the multitude of things that need examining. Things really are connected. You want to sift through everything simply and efficiently and then decide on the right combination of things you should do for your business.

> ### Strategic Tip
>
> Trying a single solution to complex business problems is like trying to build a house with only a hammer. You can pound nails, of course, and you might be able to set a few screws, but cutting lumber to length with a hammer will be far from efficient or effective. Building a house is complex; you need a master plan and a good tool set to be successful. Building a business is no different.

When creating a strategy, you need to consider many facets of the business, but you don't need to make it complicated. You need to analyze both broad, general aspects and narrow, specific details in order to make your business do what you want. A mistake many businesspeople make is to judge the quality of a process by its complexities. People seem to think the answer has to be either complex or the silver bullet—one or the other. The real answer is to craft a strategy that's comprehensive and detailed, but not complicated.

Think of it as being at a high level looking down at everything and sifting very quickly through all the noise to get into the details of the things that matter. You need to see it big at first. Then, you need to move into the important details. The next step, of course, is to do those things that matter very well. And finally, occasionally, go back up to that high level to make sure everything is still on course.

It can seem to be a tough dance along a semantic line, this stuff about comprehensive and detailed but not complicated. But when you understand it, it's an epiphany. It really doesn't have to be complicated and, as you gather information to make intelligent decisions, you'll discover that you don't need *perfect* information. You need *good* information.

You also need good *people*.

Getting People on Board

The vision will come from people. Somewhere in your collective imagination is a bright picture of the future. It's a wonder and if you craft it and nurture it carefully, it can become reality. That's what leadership in business is really all about. Dreams do become reality, when you work for them.

Simplified strategic planning can take you to your version of the Promised Land. When you plan right, you will know your version of the Promised Land and you will have a roadmap. The process gives you and your team a sense of intention and a sense of mission. This process almost always generates enthusiasm and commitment because it offers members of your team a real chance to participate in determining their future.

> ### Tales from the Strategy Vault
>
> 19th century Prussian General Helmut Von Moltke said there is no plan and no amount of thoroughness that will survive contact with the enemy. In other words, once the Prussian army met the French army, the elaborate battle plan was at the mercy of the action at the front lines. His point was that a certain level of planning is useful, but beyond that you need to develop the leaders in the trenches so they can react to fluid and uncertain tactical situations.

Of course, there may be some skeptics—and a few people who fear what the future may hold for them may be downright hostile to the idea. Questioning the status quo often disturbs those with vested interest. But we will work through the details of managing these difficult people in the next chapter.

This simplified process will produce a strategic plan—a vision of how to optimize the potential of the company—but it's also likely to have other far-reaching benefits for the organization. When there's a plan, people feel in control. They feel less anxious, more confident about stepping up to opportunities and managing threats. Priorities and efforts within the company become more focused and aligned, reducing friction and increasing productivity. In short, the plan tends to build motivation, enthusiasm, and commitment throughout the company.

Document or Tool?

Many people think of a strategic plan as a document. True, in many cases a plan is written down, but a piece of paper does not bring much in the way of benefits. A good strategic plan is really a management tool. A plan should not be a document that is placed on a shelf and revered. That's not strategy. Strategy takes a grand vision and turns it into something useful. It should be a simple state-ment of the few things we really need to focus on to bring us success as we define it.

> **Strategic Tip**
>
> A plan is useful if your managers want to pull it down from the shelf and review it every two to four weeks. If it's full of information and not just words, people will use it.

Simplified strategic planning is specific and detailed, but not excessively so. The idea is not to build a huge plan that no one reads. The idea is to build a good plan that works, is easy to understand, and is comprehensive but not ponderous. It should capture the imagination and vision of the company and inspire everyone to do their best to achieve success.

Figure 1-2. Don't do planning like Dilbert's company
DILBERT © United Feature Syndicate, Inc. Reprinted by permission.

Decide to Decide

So what are you waiting for? It's time to decide. Are you going to sit back and accept what happens? Or do you want to study your environment and understand your situation so you can take action for a better future? Do you want to realize your vision of the future? The choice is yours. You can continue along an indifferent path to *whatever*—or you can choose where to go and how to try to get there. Strategy helps you envision the future and then attain your vision.

> ### Strategic Tip
> The biggest reason companies don't do strategic planning is that they never get around to it. They let other urgent, but often less important things get in the way. Don't let this happen to you. Decide to go forward. Set dates, create a schedule, and get going.

Sometimes people finally decide to make a change when something forces them to make the tough decision to move beyond what they've always done. Other people are smarter: they recognize when a crisis is coming and change before the drama unfolds. In any event, it's time to decide on the right direction for your ship. OK, captain, assemble some good people and set sail for your future with purpose. You'll find that it's worth it. With strategy, you can determine your destination and get everyone on board moving the ship in the right direction.

> ### Outside the Meeting
> Establish a start date for strategic planning. We recommend two days for your initial planning meeting. Go out a month or two to find a date that avoids distracting conflicts. Mark the date on your calendar. **Do it *now*!** Then, after reading about the process flow in Chapter 3, schedule the rest of the meetings.

Strategy teaches you to design results. That's right—with simplified strategic planning, *you* decide the future.

chapter 2

Create a Great Strategic Team

STRATEGY DOES NOT COME FROM A VACUUM. It comes from people. Getting the right group of people involved in the process is the essential first step in the process. Strategic planning involves work and gathering information, but it also requires brainpower. You should assemble the best people in your company to create your strategic plan.

Although it may be tempting to involve as many people as possible, that's not a good idea. Nor is it smart to limit the team to the boss and a few "yes people." Strategic planning is serious business, and you need the benefit of a variety of perspectives. It's a matter of balance: keep the team to a reasonable size while reaching out for many perspectives. Your strategies will be much more robust and useful if you carefully select the people for the strategic planning team.

More than One

If you sat down by yourself to do strategic planning, you could probably come up with a lot of answers in a short time. It would be very efficient, since you wouldn't have to discuss anything, but probably not very effective. The truth is that you should spend a little more time and involve people with other perspectives. There are two reasons for this.

First, you want *input*. You cannot make a competent decision without good information and a variety of participants will provide a much richer set of perspectives.

Second, you need *commitment* from your people to make strategic planning work. The commitment of key people in an organization to a strategic plan ensures that the company will move in the direction defined by the strategy. Inclusion and participation are the best ways to build commitment.

Who Should Be on the Team?

Team size is important. You want enough people to give you a variety of perspectives but not so many that the process is difficult to manage. Generally, group dynamics are optimized with a planning team of six to eight participants. Of course, sometimes the situation is such that you must have more or fewer than that number. Don't include the wrong people or keep the right people off the team just to have "the right number."

But whom do you choose?

First of all, the CEO (or president, general manager, or whoever is "top dog") must be part of the strategic planning team. The CEO is there not just to bless the process, but to participate. More than anyone else, the CEO is responsible for setting the course for the enterprise. Trying to do strategic planning without the active involvement of the CEO will most likely lead to frustration and failure.

On the team you also want the people whose input and commitment are essential to the strategic plan. Those who report to the CEO are natural candidates for the planning team, but there are other things you need to consider before inviting everyone who directly reports. You want a variety of personalities, backgrounds, and thinking styles—and people who will express their thoughts.

> **Strategic Tip**
>
> Share information. If you involve people in the strategic planning process, they need to know about the company so their opinions are more informed. There are companies that are afraid to give out financial information but then ask people to get involved in the strategic planning process. That's like asking someone to drive your car blindfolded.

When you put together a strategic planning team, strive to build in creative and natural tensions, as shown in the major perspectives of the tension triangle. The idea is to represent the realities of the company in the planning team, so that tensions are surfaced and resolved. The three areas you must cover are operations, finance, and the market.

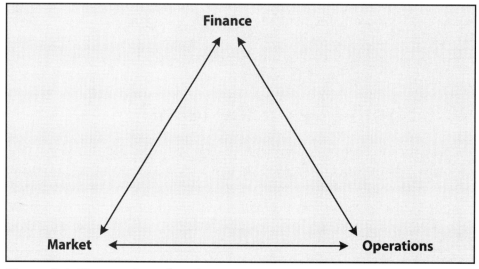

Figure 2-1. The tension triangle represents realities every business faces

Each of these perspectives represents irrefutable realities that any company must deal with. For instance, an operational reality is that you can't deliver a product if it hasn't been made. A reality of finance is that if you sell a product or service for less than it cost you to provide it, you're going to get into trouble. And a marketplace reality is that if you deliver less than the customer wants you probably won't keep that customer for long. Ignoring any of these realities will ultimately lead to trouble.

It's quite natural for a manager with the market perspective to argue for including more things the customer wants, while the financial perspective tries to take things out to improve profit. As the operational perspective rightly seeks greater efficiency, it may create tension in the organization by consuming financial capital and shifting burdens to the customer. When selecting your team, you need to reflect all of the realities and tensions in the company in order to come up with a balanced and workable strategic plan. Figure 2-2 shows the kind of people who should participate.

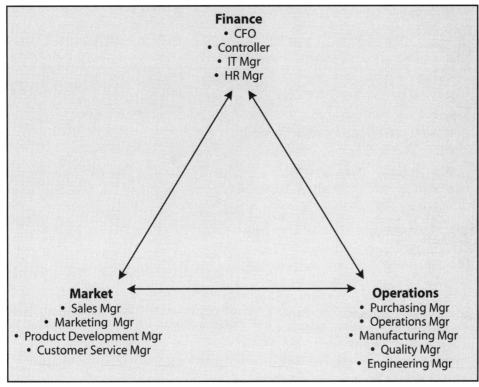

Finance
- CFO
- Controller
- IT Mgr
- HR Mgr

Market
- Sales Mgr
- Marketing Mgr
- Product Development Mgr
- Customer Service Mgr

Operations
- Purchasing Mgr
- Operations Mgr
- Manufacturing Mgr
- Quality Mgr
- Engineering Mgr

Figure 2-2. Consider including at least a few representatives from each corner of the the tension triangle on the strategic planning team

Although you should limit the core planning team to six to eight people so that it doesn't turn into the corporate equivalent of congressional hearings, you want to include others indirectly to help gather information. If people know that the information they contribute will help the team form a strategy, they can feel a part of the process even if they are not on the team. In addition, you will almost certainly need other people to support implementation of the objectives in your strategic plan, so be sure to take steps to build their input and commitment.

Who Should *Not* Be on the Team?

The rule is simple. The team should not include people who do not have a direct influence on the course of the company and a day-to-day responsibility for that course.

In working with companies, we've developed a list of the most frequent violators of this rule:

- Absentee board members
- Absentee owners and family members
- Very senior employees with no management responsibility
- Subject-matter experts who lack general company interest
- Random employee representatives
- Junior family members who wouldn't otherwise be there
- Customers and suppliers
- People with titles that sound strategic, but entail no strategic level responsibilities

> **Strategic Tip**
>
> Don't put people on your strategic planning team for political reasons. If someone is on your board because he or she is active in the community, that's not a reason to be on the strategic planning team. You want people who are directly involved in making management decisions for the company.

You may want some input from these people, but you can get it without putting them on the strategic planning team. You need people on the team who can step back and see the big picture. Anybody who cannot do that should not be on the team.

You will need people who are able to vigorously represent their perspective, but willing to compromise in order to come up with a good strategy. People who will be successful members of a strategic planning team are able to put the interests of the company ahead of the interests of their own departments.

> **Strategic Tip**
>
> If you want to include the perspective of your workers, you should think about including someone from human resources. This person should be able to give you some perspective on training, workforce motivation, safety, and other issues that affect workers. Don't include labor representatives in your strategic planning process to get this perspective. There may be important and appropriate strategic directions that a labor representative will—correctly, given his or her duties—try to resist.

The Power of Perspective

There are a lot of issues to consider in strategic planning and you should examine each of these from a lot of angles. It's simple: strategy comes from people and people have different perspectives.

Strategic planning is a vibrant process that is intended to encourage people to constructively challenge each other. You want differences of opinions and you get that by finding people with different perspectives and different personalities. Some people are creative and some

are analytical; make sure to have both types on your team. Team members are there to give their opinions, to provide information and input, and to encourage other team members to have an open and frank discussion.

Getting Your Team to Believe in the Process

If people don't believe in the process, it's not going to work: plain and simple. So how do we get doubters on board?

Initially, not everyone will believe. It's quite natural to have skeptics, those who have been through a similar process that failed to deliver and left them disappointed. If you can demonstrate to a doubter that the process can really bring improvements to the company, you may be able to make some progress. It's usually sufficient to explain this particular approach with its orientation to simplicity and tangible results and make an impassioned appeal to "give it a try."

There may also be people who do not believe in anything, no matter what you do. Remember that saying, "One rotten apple can spoil the barrel"? These people can poison the process. If they come into your strategic planning team determined to make it fail, they will succeed. Be aware of the danger that these people pose to your goals.

There have been a million books written about motivating employees; this is certainly not one more. But we stress this point: the people on your strategic planning team must believe that the process will work or you're simply spinning your wheels. Everyone we know who hasn't gotten rid of the bad apples has regretted it. That's all there is to say about that subject.

> ### Strategic Tip
>
> Beware of those who are intent on keeping the status quo because they like the way things are. For instance, if a salesman is comfortable selling into a mature market with a good margin and a bunch of loyal customers, he's probably not interested in making any changes. You need to teach people like this that change is inevitable and desirable.

But the people who can be reached must be reached somehow. How? Through a sense of urgency. When people realize that the old recipe doesn't work anymore, they're more receptive to trying something new. For example, when there's suddenly a 20% drop in sales, people realize that this is serious. Maybe you don't have a crisis now. But if not, there's probably one coming. You and your employees probably don't see it coming, but if you cast the argument for strategic planning in terms of avoiding a crisis, you have a good chance at getting people to believe. When people think that they're in danger of getting slammed somehow, they're willing to consider doing the work that strategic planning requires. Urgency is a key motivator.

Who Should Lead the Team?

Strategic planning is a process that must be led by someone. Many intuitively think that the head of the company should lead the process. Leading a strategy process is much different, however, than leading the company and, in most cases, it would be detrimental to the process for the CEO to lead it. The CEO needs to participate and voice opinions. However, if the CEO is giving opinions while trying to elicit opinions from others, his or her teammates could feel intimidated into simply agreeing with the CEO. And that could be a big problem.

The CEO is in charge of strategy-setting leadership. Since the CEO is responsible to the owners of the company, he or she is the one who will make a decision that can't be reached by consensus. Simply put, the buck stops there.

But that's different from a process leader, who should be neutral. Once you've put together your high-charging team that covers the key perspectives, you need to find someone to harness those people and help them move forward toward putting together a strategic plan. Thus, you need a process leader.

PROCESS LEADERSHIP CHECKLIST

A good process leader should be able to:

❒ Help the team focus on content by taking full responsibility for managing the process.
❒ Act as a sounding board for information, thoughts, and ideas.
❒ Help the team avoid making errors that are either conceptual or process-oriented.
❒ Help the team make sure to cover everything that needs to be covered.
❒ Keep the team on schedule and move meetings along.
❒ Tone down overly dominant personalities and make sure that any disagreement gets expressed.
❒ Ensure a realistic understanding of resource requirements and availability.
❒ Challenge the team.

Insider or Outsider?

So where do you find a good process leader? Well, you can look inside your company for someone who's capable of being neutral and managing the personalities on the team, or you can go outside your company for a top-notch professional who can fill the role. In either case, you should carefully consider the skills required for this role and make sure that you have an effective leader before you proceed.

If you have a qualified insider,

> **Strategic Tip**
>
> Don't use an industry expert to lead the process. Such a person will tell you everything he or she has learned from your competitors, and then go on to tell everything about you to your competitors. In the end, this person will lead you to adopt the same strategy as your competitors—and that's a sure way to make less money.

you'll certainly save the expense of bringing someone in. But remember there's a hidden cost. The role of the leader is to shoulder the burden of managing the meeting, freeing the others up to focus on content. So, whoever you select as a leader will have a considerably diminished role in formulating the content of the plan. Essentially, if you have someone inside your company who meets the above criteria and whose contributions to the content are not essential, you should probably appoint that person as leader.

However, an outside person brings a fresh perspective to your company that can be quite valuable. An outside person doesn't know about sacred cows and so may be more willing to ask tough questions that an insider may automatically avoid.

Outside the Meeting

Look at your list of team members and evaluate each against the above criteria for process leadership. Then consider if you can afford to have the top candidate take a reduced role in the content of the plan, or if you should consider someone outside the team. Then decide on your process leader.

Of course, if you bring in the wrong outsider, he or she can waste a lot of time challenging stuff that's simply right and doesn't need to be challenged. The wrong leader won't know when it's time to challenge. The wrong leader won't be able to read the team.

The right leader understands the process and will lead the conversation along. And the right leader understands his or her role—to lead the process, not to set the strategy. A good leader doesn't give answers, but instead helps the team find its own answers by asking the right questions.

chapter 3

Learn the Simplified Process

THERE ARE THREE QUESTIONS THAT LIE AT THE HEART OF BUSINESS STRATEGY:

- What are you going to sell?
- Who are your target customers?
- How can you beat or avoid the competition?

If you can answer those three questions well, you have a strategy.

These may seem like very simple questions that most companies should be able to answer on the back of an envelope. But try this: dangle those questions in front of eight managers in your company and then ask them to answer them specifically. Compare the answers and you may find you have the equivalent of a strategy of chaos.

There's no denying that the simplified process involves complex issues. But finding your course and direction doesn't have to be painful. It can, in fact, be fun and interesting.

But the process involves digesting a lot of information and it requires some fairly difficult analysis. Good strategic planning should be *simplified*, not *simplistic*.

The Three Key Questions

The process of strategic planning is a step-by-step approach to answering the three key questions at the heart of the matter:

- What are you going to sell?
- Who are your target customers?
- How can you beat or avoid the competition?

The first two questions define the breadth, scope, and focus of your business. First you must decide what you will do or will not do, and then you must decide whom you will serve in the marketplace. These questions help you determine an appropriate focus.

We've found that many companies do not want to be focused and seem to avoid narrowing things down. The leaders of such companies usually can't stand the idea of not pursuing a sale. If you ask the question, "What are you going to sell?" such leaders often answer, "Everything." That's not focus. That's a pursue-everything approach. Those leaders will also answer, "Everyone," to the question, "Who are your target customers?" The problem with these two answers, of course, is that there's a third question—and that question requires an examination of your resources. If you're trying to sell *everything* to *everyone*, you'll need an awful lot of resources.

It's that third question that brings a sense of realism to your strategic plan. When you get into the third question and begin examining your competencies, strengths, capabilities, and infrastructure, you'll really understand the importance of focus. You simply cannot profitably sell everything to everyone. Instead, you need to focus on applying specific capabilities to target markets. This will allow you to use your resources to your advantage instead of just using them up.

These questions are the heart of the process because at each step along the way you'll be working toward answering them. As you do, you and your management team will learn and grow. And as you learn and grow, you'll create a well-considered plan. In the end, you'll have a strategy that works and gives specific answers to those three key questions.

Culture Counts

You know what kind of employees you want. You want people who care, who really give their all for the company because they believe in their coworkers and because they believe the success of the company is good for them. You want people who will be excited about their day-to-day duties so that they pay full attention. If what they're doing is vital, useful, fun, and interesting, they're likely to pay extra attention to doing it right. In other words, you want people to take pride in their work. If people think what they're doing is dull, you're not going to get 100% of their effort because they're just going to mentally check out. The problem is a problem in all jobs—an assembly line worker in a manufacturing plant, a telephone operator in a hotel, or the CEO of a *Fortune* 500 company. Whenever somebody checks out, it can mean trouble for the organization.

That much is clear.

It's also clear that the people on your planning team need to really care about the process. It won't work if they simply go through the motions. They'd better not check out or you're in trouble. You want people to believe that this process is really going to work and they need to see that the leaders of the company believe in the process. Planning takes effort—and not just the effort of doing the research. It takes mental effort. You're going to have to think, and to really think right—responsibly and creatively—you need to care. And so does everybody on your team.

A good positive culture in the process is one in which people are

> **Strategic Tip**
>
> Perfect information isn't perfect if it takes too long to get.

excited about what you're all doing. It punches all the right buttons so people look forward to the process and to the meetings and get excited by the prospects of improved results. A good positive culture is a support for the entire process, making it challenging and fun.

A negative culture does the opposite. If you turn strategic planning into a meat grinder and you demand that everything be known in infinite detail before you ever begin to even think about making choices, people will lose interest very quickly. If you want to turn the process into a real cauldron where people just shut down and don't think about strategy, you can do that just by demanding *perfect* information.

Instead, you want *good* information. Information that helps you move toward intelligent decisions is the best kind of information. In more cases than you might expect, it doesn't have to be exact. You don't want a frivolous gathering of trivial facts; you want information that will help you get results. Results are what make the process fun. When you move forward, it's good for everyone. Each purposeful step toward your goal should be a joyous step for your team.

Structure

Good intentions alone don't get the job done. We've seen many companies that intend to put together a strategic plan, companies that have been really working at it for a long, long time, companies that really want to *do the right thing*. But for some reason the plan still doesn't get done. Such companies haven't really figured out how to do it yet. We often hear comments like these from managers in such companies:

- Perfect information isn't perfect if it takes too long to get.
- We've been kind of wandering around and discussing this and that, but it seems we're always dancing around topics. We're not actually settling down and getting to answers.
- We can never remember from one year to the next what we've actually discussed or decided.
- The discussion circles and hops from topic to topic—competitors, financials, market, opportunities, technology—and every topic is just another topic.
- We just talk about whatever comes up. It's almost like daydreaming.
- It's so complicated that we get lost.

We've heard a lot of reasons why people don't get a strategic plan together. A major reason is that they do not have a sound structure in place for doing it. If you throw a bunch of creative people from a company in a room and tell them to think about the future without any framework, the discussion will hop from topic to topic. Each player in the discussion will bring forth a perspective and a bias and it will go nowhere, because without structure each perspective weakens the process by pulling it in a different direction. With a structure, on the other hand, that individuality becomes a strength.

A structured process will ensure that you cover all the bases. It also enables you to look back and find information that you covered in your previous planning. Structure will allow you to go back and find what you thought about your competitors a year ago, for instance, and compare that with what you think about them now. When you follow a simplified structure, you are sure to examine the most important things without wasting time. You'll find that a simplified structure is a very effective way to create a plan that is concise, easy to follow, and answers the following critical questions:

- Where are we?
- Where do we want to go?
- How do we get there?
- How much does it cost?
- When do we arrive?
- Who is responsible?

After you've done the planning, you've got to do the work. After your first set of planning meetings, you should return to the plan on a regular basis, review it and figure out new objectives. When you do this, you will find that the information you gather will be better, your decision-making will improve, and the strategies you define will be more refined. The structure is set up so that this recursive process works better each time you go through it.

The Process of Simplified Strategic Planning—How It Works

A strategic plan is not a discussion about some far-off, distant dream but rather a process that you learn from, grow with, and use to find your company's course and direction. There's a lot to do, but it's not complicated. It is, however, quite specific.

At the broadest level, the process is a series of structured meetings. You start by gathering some basic data and facts without making any judgments. Then, you try to build a consensus about some assumptions for the future—again, without making judgments. After you've researched the necessary facts and developed assumptions, you sit down and review them as a team and make sure everyone understands and agrees. This is a central part of the process, because this information shapes all further discussion about strategy. The information will help to answer the three key questions:

- What are you going to sell?
- Who are your target customers?
- How can you beat or avoid the competition?

Resolve the questions in theory and then commit to resolving them in fact. Use your information and talk about its implications for your company's strategy. And once you've discussed that, you'll identify some issues that affect strategy. From there, you go forward, identifying a strategy. First you define direction. Then you define goals and objectives. Then you get into the questions of implementation:

- How do we get there?
- How much is it going to cost?
- When do we arrive?
- Who is responsible?

The entire process is much like a funnel: everything flows from the general to the specific through this series of meetings (Figure 3-1). It's far better to start with items that are more general, factual, and easy to agree upon, and then, as you reach consensus on these items, to move on to items that are more specific, future-oriented, and difficult to agree upon. One of the benefits of this structure is that it will be much easier to get your team to agree on general items first and specific items later. This will dramatically reduce the time wasted on arguments later in the process.

> **Tales from the Strategy Vault**
>
> *Just like everybody* is the proper way to describe a generic mission statement. They generally read like this:
> "XYZ Company is committed to being a technical leader in its field. We provide value to our customers by offering the highest levels of quality and service at reasonable prices. We intend to make a fair profit so that we can reinvest in our products, ensure a highly motivated work force, and provide a fair return for investors."

An example of this benefit is the mission statement. Many people have questioned why we don't put the mission statement first. Most planning processes present this as a place to start, but we've found that pursuing a mission statement first is almost a sure way to waste time. It's not unusual to hear of companies that spend days or even weeks defining their mission statement. To avoid this, the simplified process works in an orderly way. In

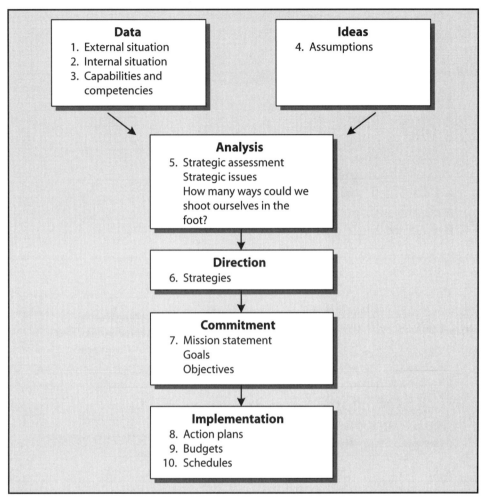

Figure 3-1. The simplified strategic planning process flowchart

simplified strategic planning, you should make sure that everyone agrees on the underlying information and assumptions about your business before you start trying to explicitly define your mission statement. If you try to put together a mission statement before gathering information, either the resulting mission statement will be generic or it will take a very long time to develop because you need to agree on the underlying information first. And you probably won't even have that information. If you do the mission statement later, at the right time, it will just flow out naturally in a minimum of time.

The process flow in simplified strategic planning is pretty concise—eight items covered in three meetings (Figure 3-2). The first meeting is two days, the second is three days, and the third meeting is two days. In the end you will have:

- Gathered information
- Assessed capabilities
- Made assumptions
- Made strategic assessments
- Formulated strategy
- Established goals and objectives
- Formulated tentative action plans
- Finalized action plans

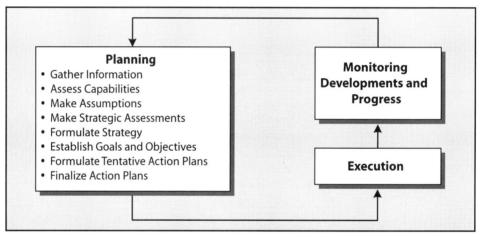

Figure 3-2. The process flow in the simplified strategic planning process

And, of course, the process is recursive, so you should do it again a year later to find out where you've been and what you want to do next. The point of the process is to make the plan manageable. If you want to create a beautifully bound 800-page bookend that everyone has and no one uses, you'll probably need a lot more meetings (just to design the cover). But if you want to create a plan—a real, workable plan that everyone can relate to quickly—this process is for you.

1. It starts with *situation analysis*, understanding your current situation and what your assumptions might be going forward.

2. Then there's *strategy formulation*, making decisions based on those inputs.
3. Finally, there's *implementation planning*, taking your decisions and driving them home in the organization to get results.

Remember: the reason for simplified strategic planning is to get results. Implementation must be specific; otherwise, it will lack vigor and vitality. Simplified strategic planning leads to specific implementation of a strategy. Dream it and then do it. That's how it works.

Take Time Deciding—Strategy Is the Big Stuff

Thinking is a very underrated skill. In strategy, you're dealing with significant issues, so it's important to take some time between meetings to do three things: gather information, digest information, and do your job.

If you try to gather information quickly, without some thought as to what to gather and how to gather it, you may miss something. Poorly prepared "homework" (the assignments done between meetings) can lead to shoddy decisions in your strategic planning meetings.

Thoughts percolate as we digest information. It's not always as smooth as we'd like, this digesting. But if you think long enough and hard enough and with enough enthusiasm and energy, you'll find answers. But you can't do the best strategic thinking when you're under time pressure. Remember, too, that you have your regular job to do. Failing to preserve time for your normal responsibilities is a sure way to create a crisis, and this is a significant detriment to any strategy process.

Because you need to gather information, digest information, and do your job, we recommend taking about six to eight weeks between meetings. Although you'll probably be able to sketch out action plans on a napkin when you get to the implementation stage, you first need to back up and consider resources. Do you have sufficient resources to do what you want to do? If not, can you find the resources necessary?

In total, the simplified strategic planning process works out to about seven days of meetings, spread out over 12 weeks so that it won't interfere with day-to-day business (Figure 3-3). (With practice and experience, subsequent cycles

PLANNING SCHEDULE   Date: _____

Worksheet No.: 9.3

Date	Session Content	
Jun 1-2	**Orientation and Situation Analysis**	**2 Days**
Day 1 AM	Orientation Identify Market Segments Served Identify Competitors	
Day 1 PM	Make assignments (see list below) Examples of selected assignments (1.1, 1.2, 4.1, 4.2)	
Day 2 AM	Idenfity current STRATEGIC COMPETENCIES (3,2) Identify and evaluate PERCEIVED OPPORTUNITIES (4.4) Assign OPPORTUNITY SCREENING WORKSHEETS (4.5-x	
Day 2 PM	Assess capabilities	

Assignments for Next Session

MARKET SEGMENT ANALYSIS (1.1-1 through 1.1-n)
COMPETITIVE EVALUATIONS (1.2-1 through 1.2-n)
ASSUMPTIONS FOR MARKET SEGMENTS (4.1-1 through 4.1-n)
COMPETITION ASSUMPTIONS (4.2-1 through 4.2-n)
TECHNOLOGY ASSESSMENT (1.3)
SUPPLIER MARKET ASSESSMENT (1.4)
CURRENT ECONOMIC SITUATION (1.5)
SIGNIFICANT REGULATIONS (1.6)
OTHER IMPORTANT ASSUMPTIONS (4.3)
BALANCE SHEET (2.1)
FIVE-YEAR OPERATING STATEMENT (2.2)
MEASURES OF SUCCESS (2.3)
PROFITABILITY ANALYSIS (2.4)
OPPORTUNITY SCREENING WORKSHEETS (4.5-1 through 4.5-n)

Date	Session Content	
Jul 18-20	**Strategy Formulation**	**3 Days**
Day 1 AM/PM	Review assignments and issued worksheets Identify and evaluate PERCEIVED THREATS (4.6) Develop INDUSTRY SCENARIO (4.7) Develop WINNER'S PROFILE (4.8)	
Day 2 AM	Complete STRATEGIC ASSESSMENTS (5.1)	
Day 2 AM/PM	Identify and evaluate STRATEGIC ISSUES (5.2)	
Day 3 AM	Identify and analyze HOW WE COULD SHOOT OURSELVES IN THE FOOT (5.3) Formulate STRATEGIES (5.4)	

Figure 3-3. The sessions of the simplified strategic planning process

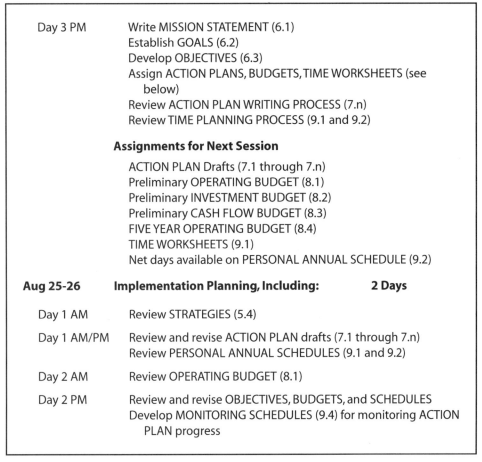

Day 3 PM	Write MISSION STATEMENT (6.1) Establish GOALS (6.2) Develop OBJECTIVES (6.3) Assign ACTION PLANS, BUDGETS, TIME WORKSHEETS (see below) Review ACTION PLAN WRITING PROCESS (7.n) Review TIME PLANNING PROCESS (9.1 and 9.2)	
	Assignments for Next Session	
	ACTION PLAN Drafts (7.1 through 7.n) Preliminary OPERATING BUDGET (8.1) Preliminary INVESTMENT BUDGET (8.2) Preliminary CASH FLOW BUDGET (8.3) FIVE YEAR OPERATING BUDGET (8.4) TIME WORKSHEETS (9.1) Net days available on PERSONAL ANNUAL SCHEDULE (9.2)	
Aug 25-26	**Implementation Planning, Including:**	**2 Days**
Day 1 AM	Review STRATEGIES (5.4)	
Day 1 AM/PM	Review and revise ACTION PLAN drafts (7.1 through 7.n) Review PERSONAL ANNUAL SCHEDULES (9.1 and 9.2)	
Day 2 AM	Review OPERATING BUDGET (8.1)	
Day 2 PM	Review and revise OBJECTIVES, BUDGETS, and SCHEDULES Develop MONITORING SCHEDULES (9.4) for monitoring ACTION PLAN progress	

Figure 3-3. (continued)

of the process can often be completed in only four days of meetings). Figure 3.3 shows the entire process. It will put you on the right track. Use your time between meetings wisely as you gather and digest information. Take time to think. And then come back ready for more.

At the end of the process, you'll have action plans that support your objectives. You allocate money though budgets and you allocate time through time worksheets. As a result, things get done on time and on budget because you have a strategy that fits the best information at your disposal. You should have in hand six to 10 action plans of things that specific individuals are going to do at specific times. They will take specific amounts of time and of money—numbers that everyone will agree are realistic commitments—and they will get things done. That's strategy with teeth.

So what are you waiting for? It's time to figure out where you're going. You have the full process: schedule your meetings and prepare to set your course and direction as you read the following chapters.

Part Two

Start by Studying the Way It Is Now

THE COURSE TO YOUR VISION, LIKE ALL NAVIGATION, STARTS WITH A KNOWN POSITION—a solid reference point. Some simple questions establish where you are. What markets do you now pursue? Who are your competitors and what is the character of the markets in which you compete? What is the nature of the business environment?

What about inside your company? How do things look? Do you know your strengths and how to capitalize on them while avoiding your weaknesses?

Finally, where is your competitive advantage? Do you have a strategic competency, a mix of skills, processes, and knowledge that offers significant value for your customer, distinguishes you from your competitors, and is difficult to copy?

Figuring out Point A is the first and essential step to charting a course to get to Point B.

So get your bearings. Where are you today?

chapter 4

Figure Out Your Markets

THERE ARE A LOT OF THINGS THAT YOU CANNOT CONTROL. Common sense tells you that your business is being affected by powerful outside forces, especially your market. The market has a powerful effect on you, but you can do something about it that is most profound. You can define your market.

Now, think about strategy. Strategic planning is about navigation. If you want to know where to go, you first need to know where you are. If you want to get from Point A to Point B, you've got be able to find both points. And to find your place in the current environment, you first have to understand that environment. The first step is to figure out what that environment is.

Many companies are trying to figure out how outside forces are impacting them, but most don't know what to look for or how to categorize things. One of the most important things you can do as you begin to evaluate your company is to break your business into understandable chunks that give you insight. A good strategy is to define your categories tightly enough so that you have a chance to dominate. If you just allow your company to be lumped in with all the others, you may find yourself controlled by some very powerful forces.

Think about a boat on the ocean. That's your business. The internal part of your company is essentially how you run your ship. You have a crew and they are efficient or inefficient and maybe good at certain things and not good at other things. These things are clearly important to you in running your ship. That's the internal stuff.

But it's equally important to know where you are and what sort of environment you face. The first question is "What are your markets?" If your ship is headed for the shoals, it doesn't matter how well you are operating. If you don't know where the shoals are, you're in big trouble. If you don't know where you are in relation to the shoals, your great operation won't do much for you.

The first step in charting our voyage from Point A to Point B is to define Point A. You can let someone define where you are or you can do it yourself.

Define Your Market

Figure out where you are. How do you do that?

Well, first you need to define your market. This sounds easy for your typical widget maker: the market is widgets, right? Well, that easy answer is often wrong. What we are after is *success*. Tackling large, broad markets makes it more difficult to win. We need to recognize that we're really making something other than "typical widgets." All widgets are *not* the same. The widget market can be viewed as a collection of niches and each niche can be dominated.

Most customers are not typical widget customers, even though most companies see a big, open-ended market. Not all customers are created equal; some will be good for you and some will be bad for you. Your company may not be what you think it is and it may not be operating in the environment that you think exists. In fact, if you look at your world differently, you can increase your power. You operate in a category. *You* can define the category any way you want. (If you don't define it, someone else will define it for you.) As the category gets smaller, your relative power in the category increases. This is particularly true if you define it to your advantage.

> **Strategic Tip**
>
> You don't have to satisfy every customer—and you don't even want every customer.

How do you define your markets? It will have a major impact on your probability of success.

No Airline Food

When Southwest Airlines decided to enter the airline industry, it took a revolutionary approach, attacking from an angle few had tried before. The traditional way to trim costs was to look at all costs and figure a way to squeeze a little more out of each. Southwest executives instead asked, "Why are we doing this?"

Suddenly, airline food disappeared, along with other stuff that just wasn't that important to a lot of travelers. How simple is this? It simply takes a new way to look at things. Open your eyes. The folks at Southwest Airlines understood that there were customers who simply wanted to get from here to there and didn't care about much else. Those customers have made Southwest very successful. Simple? Sure. And yes, Southwest gave away customers who want airline food and all that other stuff. It gave them away willingly. Southwest found the customers it wanted—the folks who don't miss airline food. And the company answered the question all the other airlines were afraid to ask—"How could people possibly fly without airline food?"

Domination Is Good

The key word in all of this is *domination*. You don't want to just *play* in the game of business. You want to *dominate*.

We're offering an interesting way to look at the world and you may have to train yourself to develop this perspective. It really is worth it. The idea here is to go against what you may have learned in most of life. In athletics, for instance, people go to great lengths to make the playing field level. After all, no one wants to watch a football game played on a field with a 45-degree slant. One team would have an obvious advantage. In business, though, we want you to find that slant.

Dominating a market may seem like an awfully daunting task for some small companies. *Dominate? But we're just a small company.* All the more reason to want to dominate.

Don't laugh. Follow along. It's not as crazy as it sounds at first. It makes perfect sense and, in fact, we know of many businesses that are dominating their markets and laughing all the way to the bank.

Dominating companies almost always have a trick up their sleeve. They don't dominate a market that is defined by someone else. They have defined a market so that it gives them a good chance at domination. The key is to have competitive advantage in a certain area so that your company brings more talent to that specific area than anybody else.

Big Fish, Small Pond

Choose your market carefully. For instance, suppose you entered the personal computer business and you managed to get 1% of the market. That 1% looks pretty good, right? After all, 1% of such a huge market is a lot of money. Gosh, what's wrong with that?

Now suppose some big PC maker decided you were too much of an annoyance and decided to just get rid of you, just swat you away. Could it be done? You bet. And when that company decides to squash you, it's goodbye to your 1%.

Let's try again and define that 1% differently. Let's say your sales, 1% of the giant PC market, are all in one particular area. Suppose you make some really great PCs that are geared to a specialty market, such as PCs rugged enough for a harsh factory floor environment. That means you've figured out how to make something better than anyone else. Now, if a big PC company comes into your little niche, it's playing on your territory. It will be much harder for that company, and maybe not worth it, to chase your 1%.

Think about it in a different way: your 1% of the PC market could be 70% of the market in one little niche. It will be hard for a competitor to displace a company that knows the niche well enough to have earned the loyalty of 70% of the buyers in that market.

See? Just thinking differently can give you a new perspective on your chances of dominating a market.

Commodity or Specialty?

One of the first key questions to ask yourself is whether you deal in a *specialty* market or a *commodity* market. Customers act as individuals, but individuals with similar behavior patterns may be grouped together for analysis.

One instructive way to group customers is to distinguish between those who show more interest in price and those who show more interest in something else.

Let's take a simple example. Look at your pen. Pens are pretty functional items. They write. Yet some cost less than $1 and others can cost $500 or more. There are $2 pens, $5 pens, $7 pens, $50 dollar pens, and so on.

So, who buys what?

Well, at the low end of the market are those who simply want something to write with. That's it. And that's a *commodity* purchase—when you'll pay for a pen that writes without skipping or blotting, but you won't pay for anything else.

All the other purchases are *specialty* purchases—when a product or service has perceived superior value that commands a superior price. And all of those different price ranges are different specialties. A $2 pen may have some added value over the 69¢ pen. It may have a little nicer design and a better feel. It may be marketed better. The $5 and $10 pens often have a significantly different feel, functionality, and design. Those things cost money and that cost is passed along to the customer. And then there's the $500 pen, which is more than a writing instrument. It's a piece of jewelry.

When people buy any pen that costs more than the lowest-price pen, they're exhibiting specialty-purchasing behavior. They want something more than just a basic writing instrument. Even the $2 pen offers a little more. It may not be a lot, but it's noticeable. And there's clearly a market for such a pen, just as there's a market for the 69¢ pen and $500 pen. And they're all different.

> **Strategic Tip**
>
> When a customer does not consider price to be the most important thing about a product or a service, that's a specialty customer.

Which customers are better—commodity or specialty? The dilemma is the classic one, between seeking high volume at relatively low margins (commodity) or aiming for domination of some niche at relatively high margins (specialty). And we've seen that success happens along a U-curve just as in Figure 4-1.

We've found that most businesses succeed at either end of the commodity-specialty spectrum but not in the middle. The middle is a gray zone—a place where customers are continually chasing the dream of the best stuff for the lowest price, customers who aren't satisfied with the high price of specialty products

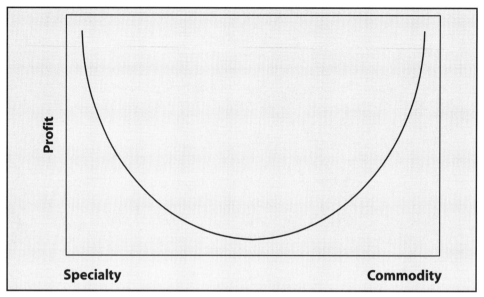

Figure 4-1. The middle point is not where you want to be

or the low quality of the commodity products. In the middle, it's very hard to satisfy the customer and make money. Yes, there are a lot of customers there, but the competition is brutal: there are a lot of companies chasing all those middle customers. Also, there's not much loyalty in the middle. It's a very difficult place to find a way to dominate.

Although there are companies that win by going for intense volume on the commodity end, we believe that it's usually much easier for mid-sized companies to dominate some specialty market niche. The best advice that we can offer is to stay out of the middle—it's almost impossible to win there.

Figure 4-2 shows some common indicators for identifying customers as specialty or commodity.

What behavior do your customers exhibit? Are they all one type? Or do you have some of each? It's important to know, because you want what you offer to be consistent with the needs and preferences of your customer.

A Story About Champagne

Once, there was a company that made champagne. The owner of this company happened to know a friend of Robert Bradford, one of the authors of this book.

Indicators	
Specialty	**Commodity**
<ul><li>Unique "product" or "packaging"</li><li>Market perceives clear superiority</li><li>Sales result from having the right product</li><li>Strong margins/profits per unit</li></ul>	<ul><li>Little differentiation</li><li>Substitutability</li><li>Sales result from low price</li><li>Weak margins/profits per unit</li></ul>

Figure 4-2. Indicators for identifying customers as specialty or commodity buyers

One night, Robert tasted the champagne and thought that the $6 bubbly tasted better than bottles that he'd bought for $20 or more. He called the owner of the fine champagne vineyard in California to tell him how much he liked the wine. When the vineyard owner heard that Robert was a management consultant, he asked if Robert had any suggestions for increasing sales. He didn't want to drop the price any lower than $6 a bottle. His profits were already very low.

Robert offered two suggestions: change the label and raise the price. The label was plain and Robert thought a fancier label would better represent the quality of the contents. He also thought that raising the price would make the bottle more of a specialty item in consumers' minds.

Think about champagne. When you go to buy a bottle, it's usually for a special occasion. At such a time, you're not likely acting completely like a commodity shopper. Champagne sales are driven by specialty behavior, so the nice artwork for the label to reach that market was money well spent.

Specialty behavior also made the higher price a good idea. Price is often used as an indicator of quality (i.e., a differentiator) in the champagne market, as many customers don't really know any other way to judge the quality of the product before they taste it.

So the champagne vintner took these two suggestions. He changed his label and he raised the price to $17 a bottle. He called Robert a few months later and reported that sales were phenomenal.

> **Strategic Tip**
>
> Sometimes, it's smartest just to declare that your product costs more. There are many memorable ad campaigns built around this philosophy. A classic was the old Curtis Mathes television ads that simply declared Curtis Mathes to be "the most expensive television in America." The unspoken message, obviously, was that the sets were worth every penny.

The key was recognizing that this had the potential to be a specialty product and then treating it as such.

Segmentation

When you set out to evaluate where you are in the world, you need to understand what parameters you want to study. Thus, you want to break your business into distinct chunks that are useful for analysis and helpful in making decisions.

The reason for this is simple. You have a fixed amount of resources, so it's important to know where it's best to apply those resources to do the most good.

> **Tales from the Strategy Vault**
>
> In the early days of World War II, both sides knew that there would be an invasion of Europe at some point. The Allies had a fixed number of troops stationed in England. They carefully kept the Germans unsure of the point of invasion, which forced the Germans to defend the entire coast of France. Then the Allies concentrated all of their resources in one area—about 60 miles of the Normandy coast. That strategy of concentrating their forces and keeping the Germans spread out greatly helped make the invasion successful. The Allies worked hard to make the playing field not level—and the rest is history.

Breaking your business up into distinct groups makes it easier to figure out what you have. How do you do this?

First, rest assured that there's no "right" or "wrong" segmentation. The point is to think creatively about your *existing* business in ways that will help you understand where you can gain competitive advantage. (We'll consider *opportunities* in a later chapter.) This will help you establish the focus for analyzing your business. In time, you can tighten up where you put your effort and resources.

There are many approaches to segmenting a business. You need to consider several of these and use them to guide you to a unique segmentation that works for your situation. Most discussions should consider segmentation along the lines of one or more of the following categories:

- Customer needs and preferences
- Commodity and specialty behavior
- Product type
- Market type
- Demographics

- Geography
- Customer type or buying channel.

One of the common mistakes many companies make when doing this is use the segmentation created by some trade association. When every company does this, it tends to put them all in head-to-head competition. This isn't good. If there are two products that are the same, the only thing to differentiate the two for the customer is the price. And when you get into a price war, it's usually a losing proposition for all the competitors.

Be creative. You want to create a segment that does not put you in head-to-head competition, but rather gives you a distinct advantage over any competition that would dare mess with you.

Strategic Tip
A reasonable number of segments is six to eight. Don't feel compelled to analyze every minute aspect of your business, only the biggest and most important. You may have some small pieces of business that are unimportant. Ignore them and concentrate on the big stuff. Your segments do not have to add up to 100% of your sales.

So how do you segment? After all, there's a lot of noise to examine in a business. Begin by studying the categories listed above to figure out what aspects are key to your existing business.

Good strategic market segments are usually made up of groupings of customers who think the same way about your products or services. It's sometimes useful to ask simple questions:

Strategic Tip
Do not include opportunities—businesses you are not involved in today—as market segments. We'll consider opportunities in Chapter 10.

- What are they buying?
- Who is buying?
- Why are they buying?
- How do they buy?
- How will they use what they buy?
- Where do we have high margins?
- Where do we have low margins?

Major differences in the answers to these questions may point to some creative ways to segment your markets.

The reason for segmentation is to make it easier for you to understand your business. This is a very individual decision for each business, but it's important that you make the effort to find the key segments of your business.

If you come up with a market segmentation in which all the segments are the same, then there's no particular advantage to looking at one segment versus another. In other words, you want your chunks to be different. You want differences between segments in key strategic factors (e.g., growth rates, profit levels, needs, competitors). Remember: this is all about domination. *You're looking for something to dominate.*

Here are some examples of how companies have segmented their businesses:

Market Segmentation Examples

Leisure Travel Business:

1. Branded packages sold through agents
2. Branded packages sold direct
3. Private label tours sold through agents
4. Private label tours sold direct
5. Consolidator remarketing

Insurance Business:

1. Commercial casualty—coastal areas
2. Commercial casualty—inland areas
3. Commercial auto—coastal areas
4. Commercial auto—inland areas
5. General liability
6. Worker's compensation

Industrial Filter Manufacturing Business:

1. Automotive filters—OEMs
2. Automotive filters—after market
3. Marine and agricultural markets
4. Shop vac type products
5. Contract machining services

Market Segment Analysis

Once you've identified your segments, it's time for some research and analysis of each so that you understand the current marketplace. Here are some specific subjects to consider:

- **Definition**. A statement of what makes up the market.
- **Needs**. There's a classic example of a drill bit manufacturer who claimed his customers needed drill bits. In fact, as professor Ted Levitt pointed out, they needed holes.
- **Preferences**. Customers don't need these, but they'd like them.
- **Total available volume in the market**. If you had 100% of the market, how much is that?
- **Your current share of the market**. (Your sales in the market divided by the total market volume times 100.)
- **What is the specialty/commodity mix in that market?**
- **Number of potential customers.**
- **Competitors' share of the market**. Identify the biggest competitors and give them credit for what they've got. Try to cover at least 2/3 of the total market.
- **Average annual real market growth rate** for the past five years. Estimate the growth of the total market, not just your sales.
- **Significant recent events in the market**.
- **Indirect competition**. This is where the drill bit manufacturer needs to consider lasers and other ways to make holes.

You need to consider this information for each market segment and summarize it for the rest of the strategic planning team to review and buy into it.

Strategic Tip

Always define growth rates without inflation. If total growth is 7% and inflation is 3%, then real growth is 4%.

Figure 4-3 is an example of a worksheet we offer and how one company used it to analyze a segment of its business. (This form and other selected forms in this book may be downloaded for internal use in your organization from our Web site, www.simplifiedstrategy.com.)

Outside the Meeting

Assign individuals on your planning team to be research leaders for each of the six to eight market segments. Each research leader should recruit several others to help prepare a market segment analysis for his or her assigned segment(s), using the worksheet in Figure 4-3. This is the first of several assignments that will be assigned to this research group (the others coming in Chapter 9). The group should complete this work and submit it to the full strategic planning team to review about two weeks prior to your second planning session.

So, where do you get this information? Well, you gather it. This is how you get your team involved and this is also where you can get employees who are not part of the strategic planning team to be part of the process.

Gathering information is one of the most important aspects of the strategic plan because the information you gather will be the basis of some decisions you make. That's why the information must be good, but it doesn't have to be perfect. The idea is to get reasonable information and then move forward.

In most cases, getting more precise information will have a cost. Some of that may be worth it, but we've seen many companies fall into the trap of seeking perfect information and then never getting around to acting. They just get caught up in gathering information.

Tales from the Strategy Vault

A member of one company attending our seminar said that they'd been doing strategic planning for about four years. We were excited and thought that the experience would bring a lot of insight to our seminar. We asked, "How is it going?" He replied, "We haven't finished gathering information yet."

The best way to gather information is to assign tasks to specific people.

At the same time, make sure that your entire organization acts as one large listening post—especially when it comes to studying the competition. For more on that, go to the next chapter.

MARKET SEGMENT ANALYSIS Date:_____
Worksheet No.: 1.1-n
Originators:_____

Market Segment Definition:
  Geographical: Ohio, Indiana, Illinois, Wisconsin, Minnesota, Iowa, and Missouri.
  Characteristics: high volume ($50MM+) manufacturers of hard candy sold through
  high-volume retailers.

Needs Served:
  Protection from crushing. Material must be clean and uncontaminated. Deliveries
  must be on time.

Market Preferences:
  Color match and consistency
  Low prices
  Stable sources

Current Total Available Volume in Market Segment: $5,000,000

Our Current Share in This Market Segment: $1,200,000 (24%)

Specialty/Commodity Mix in Market: 90% specialty behavior, very little
  commodity behavior

Number of Potential Customers:
  Concentrated market–only 5 companies

Competitors' Share in this Market Segment:
Brown 33%   National 10%
ABC 10%   Others 13%
XYZ 10%

**Average Annual Real Market Growth Rate for the Type of Products/Services We
Provide to This Market Segment over Past Five Years:**
5 years ago: $2.5 million, last year $4.6 million. Volume has doubled in the past 5 years,
  though current annual growth is estimated at only 8%.

Significant Recent Events in Market:
Largest buyer (Jones) is seeking to buy their closest competitor.

**Indirect Competition (Other Products/Services That Might Fulfill the Above Needs
in This Market Segment):**
Thermoformed plastic trays
Die cut sleeves

Figure 4-3. An example of market segment analysis

chapter 5

Figure Out the Competition and the Environment

YOUR COMPANY IS NOT THE ONLY ONE AROUND. Even your best customers don't *have* to buy from you. There are other companies that do much of what you do and your customers know all about them. When you operate in such a competitive environment, you need to have a good understanding of what your competitors are up to—not so you can copy them (a common mistake), but so you can find a way to be different. The idea is to give your customers a reason other than low price for choosing to do business with you. If you really understand this, you can be part of the ultimate win-win situation in which you, your customers, and even your competitors win. In addition to understanding competitive forces, you must also have a working knowledge of other conditions that establish the business environment. The more you know about these things, the easier it will be to craft a winning strategy.

If you know a competitor's strengths and weaknesses, you can figure out a way to position yourself to avoid those strengths and take advantage of those weaknesses. You will find that some customers come to prefer you and that you'll chase other customers away. Both results are good. If customers perceive your company as very similar to your competitors, the only way you'll be able to challenge the competition is on price. But if you differentiate your offer, you can make your competitors your "friends," as they will now tend to attract different customers from you—precisely the customers you don't want. And that's good, because it saves you a lot of energy that would otherwise be wasted in a battle for market share in an undifferentiated market. In all cases, you need information to win.

You Against Whom?

One of the most important strategic choices you'll likely have to make is determining who your real competitors are. Not just who is in your market, but who takes the customers you want. This seems simple to people who think they want all customers. But no company gets all the customers. Companies with focused strategies understand that. Strategically, you might as well get used to the idea that some customers will be yours and some won't. When you accept this fact, you can either choose which customers you get or come by them accidentally. Most companies come by them accidentally, by pretending they can have *every* customer in the market.

To choose which customers you get, you must choose which customers you will lose—in other words, who will buy from a competitor and why. This reason will tell you exactly who your real competition is. Your real competition is companies that get customers who might choose to buy from you for the same reasons you have chosen.

> **Tales from the Strategy Vault**
>
> It has been said that Southwest Airlines views Greyhound and Amtrak as more important competitors than other major airlines. The customers Southwest wants are the budget travelers who would not fly at all at higher fares. Of course, the airline is also willing to fill the rest of its planes (if any seats are left) with budget-oriented business travelers.

Think of customers you've lost in the past year or two. Of those, try to think of any that you really wished your company could have retained as customers. Why did you like those customers? Why did they leave? Which competitor(s) are they buying from now? The answers to these questions will tell you which competitors to worry about and why.

The Competition Is Your Friend and Your Enemy

In many markets, competition is cutthroat. All the competitors are after the same customers and are willing to do anything to get them. In other markets, competition has sorted out into fairly well-defined groupings—the upscale brand and the downscale brand, for example, with mainly polite dealings in a more civil competitive environment.

> ### In the Meeting
>
> Make a list of the 12 most significant competitors you face (limit it to a dozen), so you can begin gathering data on each. Drawing up the list should take less than 20 minutes at the initial planning meeting. Assign individuals from the planning team to be research leaders for gathering information on each competitor. Following the meeting, each research leader should recruit several others in the company to help gather information and complete the worksheet shown in Figure 5-1. As with other assignments, this work should be completed and distributed to all members of the full planning team at least two weeks prior to the second planning meeting.

Of course, if competitors try for the same customers as you, they are the enemy. It's simple. Not all competitors will understand the role of cooperation in competition. In fact, many will seem to be "dumb as rocks" when it comes to this. But you don't have to worry. It won't matter if your company is good at something. Look at it this way. There will be some areas where competitors can beat you and some areas where they can't. If they're going to try to beat you in a battle that they can't win, it doesn't matter how hard they try. They'll just deplete resources because you're better. They may hurt you in the short run, but they'll ultimately either go out of business or get smart. The smart competitor recognizes areas to avoid, customers to simply give away.

The strategic part of this equation, of course, is figuring out where you can win so you can concentrate all of your resources there. That's smart investing. Figuring out where you can win is, at least in part, figuring out where competitors can't win.

Market and Competitive Research

Information is power, especially in strategic planning. Informed strategic decisions are the only kinds that stand a reasonable chance of success in this global, competitive world of business. And this kind of competitive information is all around you; all you have to do is look.

But you have to know what to look for. More is not always better. Too much information can be confusing and distracting. Too much detail can be prohibitively time-consuming or expensive. In simplified strategic planning, there are some key pieces of information that you should gather on your competitors. Just try to fill in the blanks from whatever sources you can find.

Figure 5-1 shows a worksheet that we offer to help quickly summarize your analysis of a competitor. If you look down the worksheet, you'll see that we ask questions about sales performance, profitability, and growth rate and questions about distinguishing features, strengths, weaknesses, significant recent events, competitive strategy, and vulnerabilities. Be very specific and brief in your answers.

Though it may seem a daunting task to get this information, there are, of course, ways to do it. A thoughtful approach coupled with persistence usually works best. There's a lot of information that is readily available to anyone who asks or reads.

> **Strategic Tip**
>
> Precise information is not usually required in these worksheets; estimates are fine. Always test the value of getting additional information. If an estimate is satisfactory for making the strategic decision, then don't spend time or money improving the estimate. However, if you don't have a clue, don't pretend that you do. False information is worse than no information: it can lead to strategic misdirection.

> **Strategic Tip**
>
> When seeking market or competitive information, always ask where the information sought would be considered newsworthy and look there. For example, a stock analyst follows not only public companies, but also the private ones that influence the sector she follows. Information about private companies can be found in analyst reports and financial newsletters.

COMPETITIVE EVALUATION OF: *Us*   Date:_____
Worksheet No.: 1.2-1
Originator:_____

Location: Chicago

Ownership: Owned by company president, L.C. Smith

Scope of Products/Services: Interior and exterior packaging made of paper, paperboard, and thermoformed plastic.

Scope of Markets Served: Bakery and confectionery industries, also some other dry packaged foodstuffs.

Products/Services and Market Segments Where We Compete Against This Competitor: not applicable

Sales Volume: $12,000,000   **Profits:** $500,000 after taxes
Number of Employees: 120   **Growth Rate:** 21% per year

Distinguishing Features/Benefits for Customers: Clean plant, No-hassle reliability, Just-in-time delivery

Key Competitive Strengths: Outstanding market reputation, Strong technology, High level of service, Fast-turn delivery, Low debt

Key Competitive Weaknesses: Some cost/price difficulty, Must buy raw materials on open market, Although our technology is strong, it is definitely second best to Brown's

Significant Recent Events: Installation of design and testing lab

Competitive Strategy: Specialty/niche market

Vulnerabilities: Price

Figure 5-1. A sample of a competitive analysis

Some of this stuff is obvious. Things are published. It's true, all you have to do is keep your eyes open and you can find information about your competitors. There are trade journals, trade associations, and, of course, Dun & Bradstreet credit reports, which are a tremendous source of rudimentary financial information such as sales numbers, profit numbers, debt levels, number of employees, or locations. These are things that can be very interesting to you.

Other things are also published—like Web pages. These can be great sources if you just get past the obvious marketing hype and digest the one or two little nuggets that all Web pages offer. What nuggets? Hey, just log on and see what you can find. All companies are proud—and their showing off can yield valuable information.

Your People Know Things

The very best sources that you have for information about the real world are the people you employ who work in the real world. They know. They know who does what and why and when they're planning to do it again. The market is a huge resource if you just listen to your people and your people act responsibly.

Here is the word that you want to pass along to your people: *listen*.

The business world is full of people and people say things. It always happens, but if you don't have everyone in the company aware of the opportunities for sleuthing, your people may miss the obvious.

You can certainly survey your own employees to see if they know the answers to any of these questions. You may get some answers. But you get greater benefits if you create an atmosphere in which

everybody is aware of what you want to know. Then they'll always have their antennae up. If they know who the key competitors are, they can pay attention to the useful tidbits they hear as they go about their routine business. For instance:

- The HR department is constantly interviewing people. The odds are that some of those people have worked for your competitors. Whether they're interviewing for a job to sweep floors or to be VP of Finance, people will often say things about their old job that are strategically interesting. Sometimes it just rolls off the tongue. An HR person should take note if an applicant says something like: "I'm leaving my job because our company's been losing money for three quarters in a row. You know, they've gone from 500 employees to 250 over the last couple of years in three big layoffs, and my boss just left and everybody really liked working for him."

- Technical people are notorious for exchanging all kinds of information about the company in general. They are very tight-lipped about trade secrets and technology, but often open about the company's performance.
- Purchasing people may come across information if they buy from the same suppliers as your competitors. For instance, if they're trying to line up temp workers and there's a shortage, they can ask why. The answer could be that your competitor down the street is using all the temps in your area because the company is trying to enter a new marketplace. That's great strategic information and it should be recorded in your central files.

> **Strategic Tip**
>
> It's best if people inside your company gather the information. There are certainly market research firms out there that will do all of this work for you and in some areas of information they can do a fine job. But you should be cautious about handing over too much of the research, because there's intrinsic value in having your own people do it. You're after more than just the information. One of the most important by-products of this research process is the understanding gained of customers, competitors, and the general conditions of the marketplace.

The point here is to produce a competitor analysis page that outlines key pieces of information you've gathered about a specific company. You're trying to create a profile of each of your competitors.

You Live in the Business Environment

Markets and competitors are not the only factors that change and define the business environment for your company. Our experience has shown that companies need to look at other forces that shape their environment, specifically technology, suppliers, the overall economy, and regulations that affect their particular industry. These are big-picture things that create the backdrop for all business strategy. And they matter. The business environment creates opportunities and it creates challenges. If you're ready, you can take advantage of each.

In the past, a lot of companies could honestly claim these things had very little effect on them. They probably weren't correct then, but now no company around can even dare to make such a claim. These things affect how you do business, how you meet the needs of your customers, and how you make money. And when it's strategically important,

> **Outside the Meeting**
>
> For each of your major competitors, start writing a Competitive Evaluation (shown in Figure 5-1) based on easily accessible information. Then identify the holes where the information is more difficult to determine and develop some approaches to filling those in over time.

these things are part of a company's recipe for success. That is, if the situation changes, you most likely need to change the recipe. If you're ready with a new recipe for a new situation, you have a good chance to keep winning. One other thing to consider about the environment is that some changes create opportunities.

Technology Assessment

What is currently state of the art? Who has it? Consider each of the following types of technology:

- **Product**—that which goes into your product or service
- **Process**—that which enables you to make a product or provide a service
- **Service**—that which enables you to sell, deliver, or support a product or service

When you think about technology, think about how it affects:

> **Strategic Tip**
>
> In each area—technology, suppliers, economy, and regulation—there will be many factors that influence the environment. You need to sort out which of these have strategic impact on your business. In other words, if they changed, would you have to change the course and direction of your business? Take the area of regulation, for example. Many states require automobiles to undergo an annual inspection. If this regulation were abolished, it would have a significant strategic impact on a service station that specializes in inspection and repair of defects detected, but it would have minimal impact on a service station that gets most of its profits from gasoline and its convenience store. Focus on just those areas that have strategic impact.

Tales from the Strategy Vault

We have one client that makes motor couplings, a product that has been around for 100 or so years. It's an old, old product and yet the client recognizes that technology is critical. It does not affect the product, but it affects how the company manufactures it. Instead of tooling it out of metal on a lathe, they're now forming it out of powdered metal— a relatively new manufacturing technology that affects costs and quality.

- Costs
- Quality
- General availability

You should capture your current assessment of the impact of technology across all facets of your business in a one-page summary shown in Figure 5-2.

Supplier Market Assessment

Consider all of the inputs to your business. Be sure to think of not only raw materials and supplies, but also labor and service providers. Ask yourself, If the input went away, became very expensive, or suffered from poor quality or unreliable delivery, would it threaten the course and direction of the business?

Here's an example. Let's say you sell carpeting. In your town most installers are independent contractors and you need a good relationship with enough of these people in order to sell carpeting on demand. In other words, if you don't have enough installers, you're going to have to schedule carpet installations three months in the future and that's not going to help sell a lot of carpets. When people shop for carpeting, they usually want it next week, not three months from now. If you can't deliver, even though it's technically not your fault, you'll lose sales. This is a supplier market that doesn't involve materials but certainly has a strategic impact. Also consider any supplier situations where you have unique advantage. You need to list these so you can be sure to exploit them as you craft strategy.

In many ways, a primary test of viability is to have a good steady supply of whatever you need in order to do something to make money. You need stuff—whether it's labor, raw materials, supplies, services, or equipment. The people who bring you the stuff (the suppliers) are usually not machines but part of the world of commerce and thus subject to fluctuations. Supplier markets usually can affect three basic things—price, quality, and availability. So, you want to keep an eye on what affects your supplier markets because you're just one link away.

TECHNOLOGY ASSESSMENT

Date:_____
Worksheet No.: 1.3
Originators:_____

Process Technology
State of the art
- manual equipment = 1,500 units/hour with 100 ppm defect rate
- auto and semi-auto = 3,000 - 5,000 units/hour with 20 ppm defect rate

Effectiveness of technology to deliver desired product
- manual equipment–can be used to good advantage only on low-volume jobs
- automatic equipment–good for high-volume work with long runs; long changeover time
- semi-automatic machines–most effective for a wide variety of work

Efficiency (cost-effectiveness)
- manual equipment–slow and expensive; limited to low-volume jobs
- automatic equipment–fast and reliable; will handle all sizes of high-volume work; requires at least 20% market share to get reasonable 5-year ROI
- semi-automatic machines–best all-around; for middle volume with high product mix
- large work in middle volume is very expensive with any available technology

Availability/acquisition cost
- no good equipment for large work in middle volume
- only commercially available equipment is general-purpose equipment intended for other industries
- "home grown" solutions require a master tool maker on staff...few available with industry knowledge. Key asset to retain for competitive advantage.

Rate of obsolescence/useful life
- process tech turns over about every 5-8 years
- most manual equipment has a useful life of 15-20 years with modest upgrades
- automated equipment is very difficult/expensive to upgrade; 5-year life expected

Technology at competitors
- Brown is the technology leader; virtual monopoly on fully automatic equipment
- ABC, National, and ourselves are on par, but less advanced than Brown
- other competitors are "alley shops" with no technology at all

Figure 5-2. An example of a technology assessment

Service Technology
State of the art
- Fully integrated IS system
  - real-time manufacturing/inventory data to customer service
  - automated order entry from sales force with laptop computers
  - direct transfer from customer to eng./mfg. database

Technology at competitors
- we are far behind the state of the art, but so are our competitors

Product Technology
State of the art
- 100% biodegradable product with no loss of protection or anti-stick properties

Technology at competitors
- our recently patented "Green-Pak" is far ahead of all competitors

---

Figure 5-2. (continued)

Sometimes the things that affect supplier markets are not obvious. In that case, you have to look a little deeper.

For instance, if you're in a business that uses a lot of paper, the *price* of *paper* will affect your business. So, obviously, you want to keep an eye on the price of *coal*. Say what? That's right, coal. The old saying is that it used to take a ton of coal to make a ton of paper. It may not be exactly true anymore, but it is still an energy-consuming process to turn wood into paper. So if the price of coal goes up, reason says that the price of paper will too, and then so will your prices.

The same thing happens with *quality*. If you're buying materials that aren't up to snuff, the stuff you make from those materials will have a hard time reaching your standard for quality.

Finally, *availability* is a key concern. If their stuff isn't available, yours won't be available either.

You should capture your current assessment of the impact of inputs to your business in a one-page summary shown in Figure 5-3.

SUPPLIER MARKET ASSESSMENT Date:_____
Worksheet No.: 1.4
Originators:_____

CHIPBOARD

1. **Economics**
   - Many suppliers, fierce competition
   - Capital-intensive business, least attractive part of the paper industry
   - No new mills built in past 60 years
   - Running speeds have increased, giving added capacity

2. **Uses**
   - Packaging
   - Publishing
   - Products: autos, appliances, luggage, furniture

3. **Industry Growth and Pricing**
   - Growth rate = U.S. economy
   - 90%-95% capacity utilization is normal; surges in demand cause shortages and predatory pricing
   - Price increases tend to be passed through; market softness offers opportunity to negotiate better price with "hungry" mills
   - Good relationships with primary suppliers can minimize volatility in price and supply

4. **Competitive Positions**
   - We maintain three suppliers
   - Brown and ABC have their own mills

LABOR

1. **Economics**
   - Our overall wage rates are 5% lower than national industry average
   - Benefit costs are approximately 23% of wages and salaries
   - Wage increases have run slightly ahead of the inflation rate for the past 3 years

2. **Supply**
   - Supply of semi-skilled workers has dried up. We are finding it necessary to hire untrained, entry level employees and train them
   - There has been high turnover of skilled operators due to competition from the new auto plant
   - We have begun to use executive recruiters for more of the professional positions with corresponding increase in hiring costs
   - There has been little evidence of any union organizing activity

---

Figure 5-3. An example of a supplier market assessment

Current Economic Situation

There are broad economic forces that impact your business. These things also affect your strategy and decisions—such as whether to build new facilities and increase capacities or whether to shrink capacities. You also want to consider whether to push price increases or to hold the line on prices. These are questions you need to answer and you need to assess the economy in order to make smart decisions. An assessment of key economic statistics for the markets to which you sell and for the industry in which you participate is part of any good strategic plan.

> **Strategic Tip**
>
> Develop some very specific leading indicators for your industry. These will be very helpful in strategic thinking. For instance, Johnson Food Equipment makes equipment for processing chicken into cut-up pieces suitable for retail sale. This company is very dependent on the price of chicken feed: when feed prices get high, chicken gets less popular because chicken prices go up. So the company monitors the price of grain used in chicken feed, as one of several strategic indicators of demand in the industry.

There are certain broad overall indicators that make sense for most businesses to examine.

First, of course, is Gross Domestic Product (GDP), which is the value of all goods and services produced in the country you are studying. You should also look at interest rates, unemployment, the various price indices, housing starts for construction, and the capacity at which all companies are utilizing their facilities. These numbers give you a sense of the general direction of the country's economy. And you are part of that economy.

The economy is a bit like the weather. Sunny days can be followed by hurricanes in the current economy. You just don't know and, if you follow it back a couple of decades, you can find some rough spots for any industry and you can find some sweet spots. What you're looking for is simply a big-picture view of the way it is and of what you think is coming. You want indicators.

For instance, look at demographics and remember that there's a wave of the population—the Baby Boomers—who are hitting their peak productive years. There will be a series of new businesses built from this wave of creative power and it will have a general impact on the economy that should be positive if other things in other parts of the world fall into place. The globalization of the world's economy has brought in new players that could have a huge impact in certain businesses in a short period of time.

Remember that things change. In the 1970s, for instance, the world was split into the Western sphere, the Russian/East Bloc Sphere, the Chinese/Asian sphere, and the so-called Third World sphere. Now, the Russian/East Bloc sphere is just one dramatic example of how almost all of these forces have fundamentally changed. Understanding the economy is about recognizing cycles and figuring the shifts that make a difference. The key question is always: Is it going up or down? You begin to find the answer by looking at the numbers.

You should develop a list of economic statistics that reflect the broad economy and the specific markets you participate in. Figure 5-4 (page 62) is an example of the broad U.S. economic data that is available and updated quarterly on our Web site. Visit www.simplifiedstrategy.com to download the latest quarterly update of U.S. economic statistics.

Significant Regulations

Regulation can be a drag for some businesses and a bonanza for others. It all depends on your perspective.

And although the term "regulations" can sound like it's just government, we're talking about all sorts of edicts, laws, regulations, and even provisions put forth by non-government agencies that affect what you do. If someone in charge can make a decision that affects the future of the way you'll do business, then this is something that should be of concern to you.

> **Tales from the Strategy Vault**
>
> Crash safety regulations have hurt the automobile producers by increasing their costs, but the same regulations have created a whole industry to provide crash test dummies, instruments, and safety testing services.

And it can change in an instant. You can watch the machinations of government—proposing and debating and voting—and then suddenly there's a law in effect. So there you are—it's your law.

It doesn't happen often, but you need to at least keep your finger on the pulse of any regulatory agency that could make your life different. They are out there. They may never surface or they may be a constant part of your life. And they may be good for you. There are plenty of opportunities (even entire industries) that have been created because of government regulations

	09/99	06/2000	09/2000	Change from 1 yr. ago	Change from last quarter

Date:_____
Worksheet No.: 1.5

Current Economic Situation

	09/99	06/2000	09/2000	Change from 1 yr. ago	Change from last quarter
GDP in 1996 Dollars	8,905.8	9,318.9	9,382.2	5.3%	0.7%
Disposable Income/'96$	6,341.7	6,502.0	6,542.6	3.2%	0.6%
Total Personal Consumption	6,358.9	6,733.1	6,865.5	8.0%	2.0%
Personal Savings Divided by Disposable Income	1.91	0.32	-0.23	-2.1%	-0.6%
Orders for Plant and Equipment/ '92$	48.990	57.636	54.951	12.2%	-4.7%
Ratio of Inventories to Sales/'92$	1.34	1.32	1.33	n/a	n/a
Exchange Value of US$	92.9	96.7	100.8	8.5%	4.2%
Total Civilian Employment	133,650,000	135,179,000	135,161,000	1.1%	0.0%
Total Unemployment Rate	4.2%	4.0%	3.9%	-0.3%	-0.1%
Average Weekly Mfg Hours	41.8	41.6	41.2	-1.4%	-1.0%
Private Housing Starts	1,628.0	1,571.0	1,530.0	-6.0%	-2.6%
Index of Industrial Production	138.1	145.3	146.0	5.7%	0.5%
Japan Industrial Production	97.0	101.2	100.5	3.6%	-0.7%
Mfg Capacity Utilization	79.7	81.5	81.3	2.0%	-0.2%
Money Supply (M2)/'82$	4,591.2	4,791.4	4,871.4	6.1%	1.7%
Prime Rate	8.25%	9.50%	9.50%	1.3%	0.0%
30-Year Conventional Mortgage	7.8%	8.3%	7.9%	0.1%	-0.4%
Crude Material Price Index	106.8	121.2	124.4	16.5%	2.6%
Producer Price Index	134.6	138.1	139.0	3.3%	0.7%
Consumer Price Index	167.8	172.4	173.6	3.5%	0.7%
Composite Leading Indicators	105.4	106.0	105.7	0.3%	-0.3%

n/a = not applicable

All figures are in annualized billions of dollars except for Employment, Hours, Private Housing Starts, Indexes, and percentages. All $ numbers are in current dollars except as noted. Sources: The Federal Reserve Bank of St. Louis; The Conference Board

Figure 5-4. An example of a chart showing current economic situation

> **Outside the Meeting**
>
> For each area of the business environment, identify the strategic factors and describe the current situation, using the worksheets in Figures 5-2, 5-3, 5-4, and 5-5.

and there are plenty of people who are rich because the government changed the rules.

You need to have a list of the current regulations and their strategic impact (Figure 5-5) so you can monitor their development and anticipate their effect on your business.

	Date:_____
SIGNIFICANT REGULATIONS	Worksheet No.: 1.6
	Originators:_____

1. We are undertaking a safety program, at a cost of $250,000 to meet OSHA requirements.
2. The Department of Natural Resources has ordered us to provide 24-hour monitoring of effluent, at an estimated annual cost of $168,000.
3. Within 3 years, our industry will be required (under existing law) to provide FDA documentation on all food packaging. This will increase our total cost by 6%.

Figure 5-5. A list of significant regulations that affect strategy

This wraps up your view of the current external business environment, but there's more to look at. We need to assess our internal resources and capabilities. These are the topics of the next chapter.

chapter 6

Look Inside Your Company

K NOWING WHAT YOU'VE GOT IS A GOOD THING. There are two funda-mental areas to examine inside every company—resources and capabilities. Any honest evaluation requires a close look at the cur-rent financial health of the business. A sound strategy process will have you lay out your existing financial resources in a simple, easy-to-digest format. These numbers will give you a good basis for evaluating your business.

Understanding capabilities is a key concept. Capabilities revolve around the strengths and weaknesses of a company. Those can be strengths or weaknesses in any area; for example, *sources of competitive advantage, innovation, any functional area such as sales or marketing, cost struc-ture, capital resources,* or, commonly, *the management team*. If your com-pany is good at something—especially if it's better than your competitors—you should be aware of it so that you can take advantage of it. If your com-pany is not good at something, you shouldn't dwell on it. You should simply try to make it irrelevant to your chosen strategy.

Before you can craft a strategy, you need to know your capabilities so that you can take advantage of strengths and avoid your weaknesses. But to understand your resources and capabilities, you have to measure things.

Typical Measurements

We begin with "typical" measures, because, well, they're not a bad place to start. In time, however, you'll see that good strategy goes well beyond mere typical financial measures, getting to the heart of how our strategy makes us successful. But lest we get ahead of ourselves, let's look at a few of the more common financial assessments that every plan should include.

Balance Sheet. In ancient times, a country at war would take inventory of all of its military assets, such as soldiers, where they came from, and how they were positioned, so the leaders could change the deployment as the battle unfolded. For the same reason in business, you need a balance sheet—an inventory of the financial resources of the company. You don't need every asset listed and broken down in detail. You simply need a one-page balance sheet that gives broad categories on the asset side (where your resources are deployed today) and then an understanding of who owns those assets on the liabilities and equity side of the page (Figure 6-1).

Income Statement. This five-year operating statement is a historic look at the last five years of operating performance. It starts with a sales line, showing the revenue as it streams to the company, and applies the costs against it—both fixed and variable. It's usually helpful to separate those out. Finally, this statement looks at other expenses of the company, to arrive at a net income line, either before or after taxes. You want to look at these figures both in absolute dollars and as percentages over the five-year history. You want to try to find trends and soft spots or variations in revenue or expense. You want to try to understand how all of this affects the bottom-line profitability of the company (Figure 6-2).

Profitability Analysis. It's important to understand which areas of your business generate strong profits and which are weaker. Slice your business along some dimension that gives insight: by product, by distribution channel, by customer type, and certainly by market segment. For one or more of these divisions, create a table to show activity in each category, the sales generated by that activity, the gross margins from the activity, the net margins, and, if meaningful, the capacity utilization of each activity. This may take some work, but the insight it gives is worth the effort (Figure 6-3).

BALANCE SHEET AS OF 5/31/01

Date:_____
Worksheet No.: 2.1

Assets

Current Assets

Cash	57,116	
Accounts Receivable	907,821	
Raw Materials Inventory	406,539	
Work in Process Inventory	269,402	
Finished Goods Inventory	121,087	
Prepaid Expenses	115,243	
Total Current Assets		**1,877,208**

Fixed Assets

Plant and Equipment	1,923,116	
Office Furniture and		
Equipment	182,955	
Vehicles	72,399	
Total Fixed Assets	2,178,470	
Depreciation	802,711	
Net Fixed Assets		**1,375,759**

TOTAL ASSETS		**3,252,967**

Liabilities and Net Worth

Current Liabilities

Notes Payable	35,000	
Accounts Payable	284,261	
Accrued Liabilities	243,188	
Current Portion of Long-Term		
Debt	240,000	
Total Current Liablities		**802,449**

Long-Term Debt	1,440,000	
Less Current Portion of Long-		
Term Debt	240,000	
Net Long-Term Debt		**1,200,000**

Net Worth		**1,250,518**

TOTAL LIABILITIES AND NET WORTH		**3,252,967**

Figure 6-1. An example of a balance sheet

FIVE-YEAR OPERATING STATEMENT

Date: _____
Worksheet No.: 2.2

	$1996	%1996	$1997	%1997	$1998	%1998	$1999	%1999	$2000	%2000	Est $2001	Est %2001
Gross Sales	6,124,166	106.0	7,349,633	106.1	8,672,566	106.1	9,786,815	106.4	11,803,265	107.0	14,000,000	106.9
Deductions from Sales	439,276	7.6	512,746	7.4	605,711	7.4	677,285	7.4	789,745	7.2	875,000	6.7
Variations in Finished Goods & WIP	95,061	1.6	92,125	1.3	110,244	1.3	89,305	1.0	22,305	0.2	25,000	0.2
Net Sales After Inventory Adjustment	5,779,951	100.0	6,929,012	100.0	8,177,099	100.0	9,198,835	100.0	11,035,825	100.0	13,100,000	100.0
Materials	1,802,244	31.2	2,221,431	32.1	2,616,672	32.0	2,927,910	31.8	3,362,900	30.5	3,900,000	29.8
Labor	1,397,188	24.2	1,700,678	24.5	1,981,311	24.2	2,211,905	24.0	2,643,000	24.0	3,150,000	24.0
Payroll Taxes on Labor	120,050	2.1	146,127	2.1	172,536	2.1	190,445	2.1	236,240	2.1	290,000	2.2
Equipment Repairs	70,359	1.2	75,219	1.1	98,371	1.2	115,020	1.3	150,700	1.4	185,000	1.4
Manufacturing Expenses	102,039	1.8	97,906	1.4	124,292	1.5	134,600	1.5	239,210	2.2	275,000	2.1
Power & Light	40,580	0.7	48,500	0.7	65,450	0.8	81,725	0.9	97,920	0.9	125,000	1.0
Total Variable Costs	3,532,460	61.1	4,289,861	61.9	5,058,632	61.9	5,661,605	61.5	6,729,970	61.0	7,925,000	60.5
Gross Margin on Variable Costs	2,247,491	38.9	2,639,151	38.1	3,118,467	38.1	3,537,230	38.5	4,305,855	39.0	5,175,000	39.5
Supervision	68,247	1.2	75,072	1.1	82,170	1.0	84,625	0.9	104,085	0.9	120,000	0.9
Depreciation	219,638	3.6	227,199	3.3	278,021	3.4	307,600	3.3	387,357	3.5	500,000	3.8
Other Fixed Manufacturing Costs	290,447	5.0	339,532	4.9	406,078	5.0	445,765	4.8	578,570	5.2	650,000	5.0
Total Fixed Manufacturing Costs	569,332	9.9	641,803	9.3	766,269	9.4	837,990	9.1	1,070,012	9.7	1,270,000	9.7
Sales and Administrative Salaries	649,374	11.2	701,324	10.1	809,358	9.9	901,295	10.0	1,134,391	10.3	1,250,000	9.5
Advertising	62,572	1.1	65,708	0.9	73,539	0.9	89,065	1.0	79,165	0.7	100,000	0.8
Depreciation	27,927	0.5	29,323	0.4	32,807	0.4	36,975	0.4	55,000	0.5	60,000	0.5
Professional Services	36,396	0.6	48,503	0.7	64,516	0.8	74,180	0.8	97,930	0.9	100,000	0.8
Management Development	28,987	0.4	29,462	0.4	25,431	0.3	31,060	0.3	46,305	0.4	50,000	0.4
Pension	101,807	1.8	106,718	1.5	114,972	1.4	113,100	1.2	183,610	1.7	210,000	1.6
Other Sales & Administrative Costs	273,218	4.7	306,421	4.4	376,465	4.6	439,505	4.8	501,611	4.6	580,000	4.4
Total Sales and Administrative Costs	1,180,288	20.4	1,287,459	18.6	1,497,118	18.3	1,685,180	18.3	2,098,012	19.0	2,350,000	17.9
Operating Profit	497,871	8.6	709,889	10.2	855,080	10.5	1,014,060	11.0	1,137,831	10.3	1,555,000	11.9
Interest Expense	125,519	2.2	138,071	2.0	163,710	2.0	186,855	2.0	266,570	2.4	300,000	2.3
Non-Operating Expenses	6,125	0.1	7,350	0.1	8,675	0.1	8,725	0.1	9,525	0.1	14,000	0.1
Net Income Before Taxes	366,227	6.3	564,568	8.1	682,695	8.3	818,480	8.9	861,736	7.8	1,241,000	9.5
Income Taxes	126,758	2.2	198,189	2.9	238,491	2.8	269,766	2.9	297,245	2.7	550,000	4.2
Net Income After Taxes	239,439	4.1	366,379	5.3	454,204	5.6	548,714	6.0	564,491	5.1	691,000	5.3

Figure 6-2. An example of a five-year operating statement

Once you've developed this information, you have to decide whether to share it with your people. We would encourage you to do that. When you can get your employees to understand how the company makes money, and particularly understand how their jobs contribute to either making money or not making money, then most will naturally try to "play the game" to improve performance. The idea is to let employees know the financial data so they know if the company is making money or not. This is called *open book management* and it can be a great benefit in aligning your organization's culture with your strategy. One of the best books on this topic is *The Great Game of Business* by Jack Stack (Doubleday-Currency Books, 1992). *Open Book Management* by John Case (HarperBusiness, 1996) is regarded by many as the definitive text on this subject.

PROFITABILITY ANALYSIS BY *Product* FOR 2000

Worksheet No.: 2.4-n
Date: _____

	# of Trans- actions	% of Trans- actions	Net Sales ($)	% of Sales	Gross Margin on Variable Cost ($)	Gross Margin % of Sales	% of Total Gross Margin	Operating Profit ($)	Profit % of Total Profits	% of Total Profits	% of Capacity Utili- zation
Dividers	612	25	2,472,025	22	1,114,324	45	26	434,847	18	38	66
Layer Cards	428	18	1,997,486	18	602,875	30	14	10,396	1	1	77
Separators	254	11	1,169,797	11	473,367	40	11	141,243	12	12	65
Pads	288	12	1,357,407	12	488,775	36	11	76,295	6	7	82
Sleeves	198	8	971,152	9	557,450	57	13	286,068	29	25	90
Cups	154	6	728,364	7	312,217	43	7	107,655	15	9	75
Partitions	138	6	794,579	7	289,105	36	7	62,029	8	9	55
Boxes	346	14	1,545,015	14	467,742	30	11	19,298	1	2	46
Totals	2,418	100	11,035,825	100	4,305,855	39	100	1,137,831	10	100	66

Figure 6-3. An example of a profitability analysis

These are fairly common indicators of the financial health of an organization that you should consider in order to develop a successful strategic plan. In addition, there are other tangible measures that should be developed particular to your type of company. Measures such as delivery cycle times, break-even analysis, and capacity utilization can be helpful. The point is to find the short list of measurements you need to analyze your performance and your future and to avoid being distracted by anything else.

> **Strategic Tip**
>
> A key point of open book management is that it should be accompanied by lots of education. Financial data and other measures are often misinterpreted if managers don't properly explain them before sharing them with employees. Once employees understand the data and their ability to influence it, it becomes a powerful motivator of high performance.

Other Measurements That Drive Strategy

> **Outside the Meeting**
>
> Between the first and second sessions, ask your financial person to prepare a simple balance sheet (Figure 6-1), a simple income statement (Figure 6-2), and a profitability analysis (Figure 6-3) to include in your plan.

Why do you make money?

To answer that, you need good measurements viewed from several vantage points. This will get you to the heart of your strategy, to the core of what makes you successful. Viewing a business from the perspectives discussed earlier in the "tension triangle" (Figure 6-4) should help you understand why your company is successful and makes money.

So, put on your "owner's hat" and select several key measures of *financial* performance. Then, from the vantage of a *customer*, what would be the three or four key things you care about? Consider the *operations* perspective and ask what are the key indicators of internal performance.

And finally develop a set of several measures of *innovation or learning* that indicate if the company is keeping up with changing times.

But first, you'd better measure cash flow. Usually, it's lack of cash flow, rather than short-term lack of profit, that puts a company out of business.

These things that you measure can be broad or specific. If there is anything that you can measure that helps answer that question, "Why do you

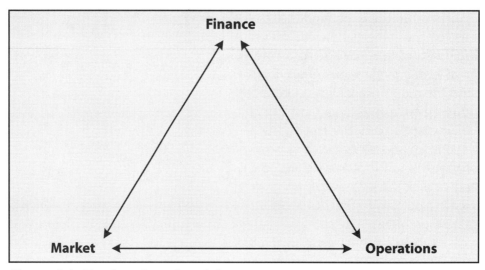

Figure 6-4. The "tension triangle"

make money?" measure it. If you make money because your costs are lower than your competitors', you want to pay attention to that. If you make money because you satisfy your customers better than others do, or utilize your capital better than others, or innovate better than others, you should develop a way to track these results. When selecting areas to measure, you want to focus on a few things. You want to measure a few key variables that drive the bottom-line results of your business.

For many of your measures, typical measurements—the kind found in most business texts (market share, sales revenue, labor efficiency, margin, etc.)—will be suitable. A few of the things you want to track may be more unusual and difficult to measure. But difficulty should not cause you to shy away from a measure; with some creative thought, a good means can be found. It's often these "unusual" measures that give some unique insight into your business and allow you to outperform the competition.

> ### Strategic Tip
>
> Innovation is a hard thing to measure, but 3M has a classic way: the percentage of sales that come from products introduced in recent years.

How, for instance, do you measure if a customer is happy?

Well, think. As a customer, when was the last time you thought to yourself, *This is great, I am really happy about this?* Can you think of what made you a happy customer and how you exhibited your joy? Did you buy again, did you refer friends, or did you purchase complementary after-market products? Though intangible factors such as customer satisfaction may be more unusual and difficult to track, with thought and ingenuity you can develop measures for these and observe the trends to give you insight into your business—insight that your competitors are missing.

It's different from the financial measures you're used to, but the truth is that you really can measure customer satisfaction—at least to

> ### Tales from the Strategy Vault
>
> 20% of the participants in the Simplified Strategic Planning seminar that we conduct for Michigan State University come because somebody else from their company has already attended this seminar. They liked it and actually told someone in their company, "Hey, this is worth the time and money to go." That's how we measure customer happiness—and we constantly strive to improve that measurement.

some degree. But in some cases you may not be able to directly measure an important success factor. In those cases, you may have to identify some of the key drivers that contribute to the factor, but this approach can be just as effective. For example, some indirect measures of customer happiness might include on-time delivery, relative price levels (for similar services), in-service product life, or warranty costs.

The key is to find something that is significant for your business and then define ways that make sense to measure that factor.

In the end, with the financials and other measurements that we're talking about here, you should come out with approximately 15 key measures to examine. You could end up with a few more or less, but don't let the list get long. If you can do a dozen important measurements well, you're on your way toward understanding a successful strategy (Figure 6-5).

MEASURES OF SUCCESS				Date:_____ Worksheet No.: 2.3	
	1996	1997	1998	1999	2000
Financial					
Sales in $	6,124M	7,350M	8,673M	9,787M	11,803M
Gross margin on sales	39%	38%	38%	39%	39%
% beyond break-even point	27%	35%	36%	39%	34%
Net profit after taxes ($)	239M	366M	454M	549M	564M
Cash flow generated ($)	134M	278M	330M	445M	484M
Return on invested capital	14%	19%	26%	27%	26%
Customer					
Number of customers	128	140	150	154	165
Delivery time (avg. days)	28	20	13	13	12
% complete on time	?	?	?	86%	94%
Internal					
Orders/inquiries	.41	.49	.66	.77	.79
Value added/employee ($000)	40.8	47.0	53.3	52.8	56.9
Scrap rate	?	?	?	4%	1%
Innovation/Learning					
% of sales from products < 5yrs old	?	?	5%	7%	13%
Number of patents filed	?	?	3	0	1
Months to break-even: new products	?	44	42	43	42

Figure 6-5. Some measures of success

You Are What You Do—Be Honest

Self-analysis is always difficult. It's easy to talk yourself into thinking you can do things that you can't, but these delusions will only offer temporary refuge. If you assume your company has strengths, resources, and capabilities that it doesn't actually have, you're going to make some really poor strategic decisions. If you wear your rose-colored glasses when planning, you will overestimate what you have and fail to deliver on your plan. It's just that simple.

Specifically, you must concentrate on being honest about your strengths and weaknesses. What are you good at?

One problem you might naturally run into is that, for instance, your vice president of manufacturing will be predisposed to saying, "We are good at manufacturing." This may or may not be true. The question is "Are we really good at manufacturing?" Sometimes it's hard to ask that question.

One of the things we've found over the years is that a lot of companies think they're good at things that they're really not so good at. It's often easy to convince yourself that you're good at something, but it is harder to convince yourself that you're not as good at something. Think of it this way: Would you ever really know it if someone were thinking about something more clearly than you were? The answer is definitely no. It's impossible to conceive of someone thinking more clearly, because one of the things that's built into humans is a strong predilection to thinking our perspective is the most reasonable.

> ### Strategic Tip
> If you're trying to be the low-cost leader in your industry, you should have some measures that reflect that. If you're trying to be a leader in innovation, you should have measures that reflect that. No matter your intention, figure out a way to measure it. If you don't measure the things that cause customers to prefer your company, you may be courting disaster.

Still, at the end of the day you are what you are. You are not what you think you are or what you wish you were. You have a particular set of strengths and weaknesses. You have to be honest in order to create a workable strategy.

> ### Outside the Meeting
> Define a total of 10-15 measures that are the key drivers of success in your business. Be sure to have a least a few from each of the key perspectives: financial, customer, internal, and innovation/learning. List these as shown in Figure 6-5. Then develop historic data for as many of the last five years as possible.

Focus on Strengths, *Not* on Weaknesses

Given a list of strengths and weaknesses, which captures your attention? For many companies it's the list of weaknesses. They focus on what's wrong with their company and try to fix it. They want to fix those weaknesses so that they can be just as good as all the companies that are stronger.

So what's wrong with that? After all, everyone wants to improve. Well, it's backwards. Every company—even successful ones—will have strengths and weaknesses. Unless a company is perfect (something that takes an infinite level of resources), it will have some weaknesses, and in many cases its weaknesses are created by its strengths. This is almost a natural law. The tortoise lacks speed due to his strong heavy shell for protection. To gain speed, a tortoise would most likely have to give up his shell. Would he then be better off? Would focusing on increasing his speed ever make him as fast as the hare? While it may sometimes be necessary to correct a *life-threatening* weakness, focusing on weaknesses is generally a waste of resources.

In business, as in nature, a far better way to use resources (time and money) is to understand where you're already ahead and try to get further ahead. Put your resources into increasing the distance from the competition and you will get more bang for the buck.

A good strategist will clearly understand the strengths and weaknesses in a situation. Having done this, you should then position the business to avoid situations where you are weak and instead focus on the areas where you are strong. You will further differentiate the company, rather than wasting time and money trying to be just like everyone else.

Thermopylae

A classic example of focusing on strengths occurred in classical times. One year, some of the scariest bad guys of the ancient world—the Persians— invaded Greece with a large army (say 20,000 men, though some historians will disagree with this number). As their army was the largest in the world at the time, they were initially quite successful.

Although Greece was falling without much of a fight to this huge army, the Spartans decided they wanted to stop the Persians. The problem was that the Spartans could field only about 2,000 men, so they knew that the size of their army was clearly not a strength. But they knew Greece better than the Persians and that was an advantage, and their soldiers were also vastly superior one-to-one.

The Spartans were ingenious. They staged the battle at a place called Thermopylae, a narrow pass on the east coast of Greece that was wide enough for maybe a column of 500 men at a time. So, the battle was even: 500 against 500 at any one time. And although it was 2,000 Spartans against 20,000 Persians, the Spartans had the advantage because they geared the battle to their strengths.

Learn from the Pig

Let's take a simple example. Let's say you have a pig. What do you do with a pig?

Well, what do you want to do with your pig? Do you want to have that pig for a pet? Or do you maybe want to put that pig on Broadway? Or, perhaps, do you want to enter that pig in a 4H contest to try to win a blue ribbon? Or do you just want bacon?

You have one pig. Those are four options:

- Pig for pet
- Pig on Broadway
- Pig in 4H contest to pursue blue ribbon
- Bacon

So, as the CEO of said pig, you analyze your options.

There are some things that are very easy to do with a pig—bacon, for instance. A pig is very good at becoming bacon with a little human assistance.

But maybe you want to raise your pig to enter a contest and win a blue ribbon. This is a little bit harder, because you have to really care for the pig and nourish it well and groom it. But if you've got the right pig, it can win a blue ribbon in a 4H contest. This is something a pig can do.

If you want a pig for a pet, you're going to have to work a little bit harder. Pigs apparently make wonderful pets, but there's quite a bit of training involved and it's probably something most people don't know much about. In other words, it's a little bit difficult. And you've got to question whether

What do you do with the pig?

it's worth it to have a pig for a pet. Maybe it is. Only the CEO of Pig Inc. would know for sure.

But if you want a pig on Broadway—as some sort of singing and dancing act—you're going to be wasting your time and annoying the pig as you try to teach it. Pigs don't sing and dance.

In business terms, singing and dancing are not the strong suits of a pig. Bacon is a strength. If you've got a pig, you already have value. You don't need to teach it to sing and dance—even if the inability to do Broadway is a noticeable weakness of the pig. Don't sweat the weaknesses. Focus on the strengths. Learn from the pig.

Finding Your Strengths and Weaknesses

So how do you find your strengths and weaknesses? The easiest and most effective way is to ask your team. Most top managers have a pretty good sense of where a company is strong or weak. Take a comprehensive look at your business and capture what you see in the areas most important to your future success.

Be certain to explore strengths and weaknesses around management, human resources, and corporate culture. These are often regarded as "too soft" for analysis, but they're some of the most important areas to understand since they influence all aspects of the business. Try to assess your strengths and weaknesses honestly, as if an outsider with good knowledge of the entire industry were making the judgment.

Understanding your strengths and weaknesses can give insight as to where to attack a competitor or where you should avoid competition altogether. That's useful for success in any particular battle.

competitive advantages	organization design
customer satisfaction	internal systems
marketing/sales performance	management
capital resources	human resources
costs/pricing	corporate culture
innovation	

Figure 6-6. Areas to consider when identifying strengths and weaknesses

But what does it take to win the war? It takes more than a collection of strengths. You need to define and amass a collection of skills that are really valuable to your customers and set you apart from the competition. You need something that makes you better or different than your competition. We call these "strategic competencies" and they're the topic of the next chapter.

> ### In the Meeting
>
> In the first planning meeting allocate about an hour to identifying capabilities. Ask your team to develop a list of the most important strengths and weaknesses of your company. Aim for a balanced list, with about the same number of strengths and weaknesses (8-10 of each). Once you have a good list, rate each for importance and performance using the two scales shown in Figure 6-7. Identify the critical strengths you want to exploit and critical weaknesses to be avoided (or possibly fixed) when crafting strategy for your business.

CAPABILITIES ASSESSMENT

Date: _____
Worksheet No.: 3.1

Strengths	Importance	Performance
Service levels	1	2
Top management is close to operations	6	1
Day-to-day management performance	4	3
Response time	3	1
Flexibility	3	2
Reputation in marketplace	2	2
Design technology	2	2
Weaknesses		
Day-to-day pressure on top management	2	7
Pressure on top management due to jobs that are continually growing and changing	2	7
Time for forward planning	2	8
Manufacturing costs	3	6
Perspective, breadth of experience outside of company	5	6
Raw material purchasing	4	6

Figure 6-7. Measuring strengths and weaknesses (continued on page 78)

Importance	Performance
1 Extremely Critical	1 Almost Perfect
2 Very Critical	2 Excellent
3 Critical	3 Good
4 Extremely Important	4 Some Strength (on the balance)
5 Very Important	5 Neutral
6 Important	6 Some Weakness (on the balance)
7 Extremely Beneficial	7 Poor
8 Very Beneficial	8 Very Poor
9 Beneficial	9 Abysmal

Figure 6-7. (continued)

chapter 7

Do It Better and Different—Strategic Competencies

IMAGINE THAT YOU'RE HOLDING A BOX THAT CONTAINS SOMETHING of great value to your customers and no one else has it or can even copy it without great difficulty. Do you think you could make any money with it? Of course you could! That's the "holy grail" in business—to have something that's both valuable and unique, something that customers really want and that makes you different from other competitors. We call such things *strategic competencies*—and you should find yours.*

But strategic competencies are not like many other things in business. You can't go anywhere and 'buy' a strategic competency, the way you can purchase a machine, acquire a patent, or even hire an employee. That's because true strategic competencies are different. They're *intellectual* assets, not *physical* assets, and they're the hidden drivers behind most successful modern companies.

---

*These are also called "core competencies" or "key competencies." The groundbreaking work in this area was done by James Brian Quinn, Gary Hamel, and C.K. Prahalad. For in-depth coverage of this topic, read *Intelligent Enterprise* by James Brian Quinn (Free Press, 1992) or *Competing for the Future* by Gary Hamel and C. K. Prahalad (Harvard Business Press, 1994).

Look at it this way. The more intellectual content you have in what you do, the better you can perform. The more you can know about designing your service, or making your product, or delivering it to your customers' tastes, or advertising it, or anything else, the more likely it is that you already have a strategic competency. You've just got to find it. If you can put your special know-how (which is better and different) into your services or products, you'll have a winner. But first you've got to find that unique and valuable knowledge.

The Mix Is Important

A strategic competency is almost never a single thing. It's almost never a skill, a person, a patent, a trademark, or anything like that. It's usually a combination, a potion, made up of three elements:

- **Skills:** A skill is any manual or mental activities that arise from talent, training, or practice.
- **Processes:** A process is any manual or mental systematic series of actions that are directed toward some end. Include any significant "know-how" resident in your company.
- **Knowledge:** Knowledge includes any information, data, or understanding of facts or principles resident in your company.

Single elements can be the source of strengths or temporary competencies but usually not true strategic competencies. In fact, strategic competency is often made up of a combination of rather ordinary elements.

A strategic competency is almost always a combination of skills, processes, and knowledge.

Tales from the Strategy Vault

It can be argued that Federal Express has a strategic competency in "small package delivery logistics." The company combines ordinary skills of flying planes and driving delivery routes with processes for automated package sorting and tracking. It adds in knowledge of weather forecasting, urban traffic patterns, and more, to arrive at very valuable and relatively unique know-how for getting small packages anywhere in the world overnight. By themselves, these things are rather ordinary, but in combination, they form a differentiated competency.

But Value, Uniqueness, and Sustainability Are Key

Any competency is a combination of skills, processes, and knowledge. What makes it a *strategic* competency is that the particular combination is also of significant value to your customers and rather unique among competing companies. It also must be difficult to copy. Otherwise, the uniqueness will be short-lived. When a competency has these attributes, it can be more than a strength; it can become a weapon that companies can use to win the battle for competitive advantage.

> **Strategic Tip**
>
> A strategic competency has to be strategic. If, for instance, you are the greatest company in your industry at the art of internal memo writing, it doesn't have much strategic value, because memos are probably not going to create much value for your customers.

A strategic competency is something that can be used over a long period of time. And it's almost always knowledge-based. It's a big stick—something that gives you clout in the marketplace. A strategic competency lifts you above the fray, it's substantial, and it gives you a sufficient and sustainable advantage in the marketplace.

Strategic Assets Are *Not* Strategic Competencies

If something of value is transient, it's probably a strategic *asset*, not a strategic *competency*. For instance, a T-shirt kiosk in Washington, DC, right across from the Washington Monument creates value for the cus-

> **Tales from the Strategy Vault**
>
> If you say you're going to see a movie put out by the Walt Disney Studio, it has a certain meaning. People take their kids to see *Disney movies*. No other studio can make this boast. What is a 20th Century Fox movie or an Orion movie? But we all know about *Disney movies*. Also, Disney has the two biggest theme parks in the country. Family movies and theme parks. That's a lot of know-how—and it all comes from the same competency: creation of family entertainment.

tomers who want Washington Monument T-shirts right there. It's difficult to copy because it's the only kiosk that the park service permits. Yet it's transient because you don't know if the people running the kiosk will keep it the next time it goes out to bid or however it is awarded. It's transient, temporary. Suppose the park service suddenly decides to allow two or three or ten other kiosks in there. Then what? But let's say you have a plan.

What if you figured a way to site and secure T-shirt kiosks adjacent to other key tourist attractions? That may involve knowledge of the key inner workings of the park system. It may involve knowledge of supplier relationships. It would probably even involve real estate knowledge so you would know how to procure sites. It would involve a combination of things, mostly knowledge-based. Now you have something more sustainable that might be a strategic *competency*.

> ### Tales from the Strategy Vault
>
> Building off a strategic competency in developing consumer personal care products, Procter and Gamble has sustained over 100 years of strong growth, even though many of its once high-flying products, such as bar soaps and toothpaste, have matured.

There's nothing wrong with having a strategic *asset*. You can make a lot of money with great assets—but only for a while. A great product, even if protected by a patent, has a finite time over which it will sustain the success of a company. Over time its value erodes as it matures and the patent protection wanes. By contrast, the know-how to develop great products (a first-class new product development process) can sustain a company indefinitely. In fact, the more it's used, the more the intellectual assets of the company improve and and the stronger the competency grows.

If you have a strategic competency, you should use it and exploit it. Unfortunately, many companies cannot identify a strategic competency—even if they have one!

Why Find It?

You want to know about your strategic competency.

You want to know so you can take advantage of it. That's what it is, an advantage. Imagine having an advantage and not really knowing about it, so you don't take full advantage of it. Got it? Good, because it may be the best lesson you will ever learn in business. If you have a competitive advantage, use it.

Four Questions

So now you are on a search to see if your company has any strategic competencies. Since most companies are lucky to have one or two real strategic competencies, you'll need a litmus test to separate strengths and strategic assets from true strategic competencies.

A strategic competency must pass four specific tests:

- Is it a combination of skills, processes, and knowledge?
- Does it differentiate the company from the competition?
- Does it create strong value for the customer?
- Is it difficult to copy?

If you don't get a resounding "yes" to each of these questions, you should be skeptical that you have a strategic competency.

One area where many companies think they have a strategic competency is customer service. Every company claims to be the best at this. Well, how can this be? *We're a customer-driven company so we have to have a strategic competency in customer service.* Maybe yes, and maybe no. More likely no. There are certainly companies that have a strategic competency around some aspect or element of customer service. But the fact that you're good at customer service doesn't necessarily make it a strategic competency. It has to pass all four of the above tests. Strengths are good, but they're not strategic competencies. We repeat: it has to score "yes" answers to the four questions.

> **Tales from the Strategy Vault**
>
> LB White makes propane-fired heaters for warming barns for farm animals. The company has developed a strategic competency around the technical know-how for designing and making very safe, efficient, high-reliability heaters. That gives the company the capability of creating products that can be operated unattended, so farmers know they don't have to go out to the barn in the middle of the night to keep the young animals from dying. The company has a deep knowledge of what farmers are facing and has set itself apart from the rest of the industry by using that know-how.

So what about value? Well, that's simple. Think about the last time you were a customer and you were really satisfied. A customer needs to think that he or she is getting a good deal by giving you money. *I can give you money? This is great.* If customers are not willing to give you money, you have not created value. Some items may add value, such as rapid delivery. But if those things are normal for everyone in the industry—table stakes in the poker game of business, if you will—then it really isn't adding unique value. Remember: it has to be different.

Finally, it has to be difficult to copy. If your advantage can be eroded or eclipsed in a short period of time, it is not a very worthwhile competency.

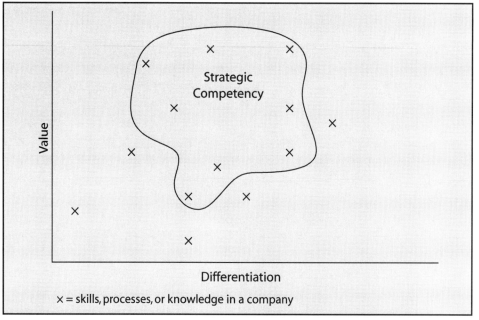

Figure 7-1. Strategic competency is a combination of skills, processes, and knowledge that is valuable to customers and differentiated from competitors. The area covered here is the combination one company identified.

Finding Your Strategic Competency

Look for clues. List all of the skills, processes, and knowledge that you have that contribute to making your company unique. Then look for combinations that may add up to something that will pass the competency test. Look at everything and see if you can get things to add up to a strategic competency. Look at skills, processes, and knowledge. Answer the questions.

Think. That's often the way to find a strategic competency that you're unaware of. Ask yourself, where and how do you win? It's often that simple. If there's a type of customer you can consistently take away from competitors, you may have a strategic competency. If you've figured a way to do something better than everybody else, customers find value in it, and it will be tough to copy, you have yourself a great strategic competency.

Of course you could raise the bar so high that you will never find a strategic competency. But that's where fairness and honesty come into play. Just as you can be too kind to yourself, you can also be too harsh. You simply have to be honest.

Strategic competencies need to keep growing. That's what sustains them. Otherwise, there is danger of being overtaken by competition. Walt Disney specializes in movies, for instance, but the organization is not simply riding on the reputation of *Snow White*. It still makes *Disney movies*. It uses its know-how over and over, getting a little better at it each time.

Strategic competencies stem from your company's intellectual attributes. They may or may not last forever, but they tend to endure and sustain a company for a very long time. And they generally improve or become more valuable as they are used.

> ### In the Meeting
>
> During the first planning session, you should allocate about 90 minutes to determining your current strategic competencies. Begin by identifying major accomplishments in the organization that have brought significant increases in market position or customer mindshare. Try to identify any skills, processes, or knowledge that helped bring about the success. List these as shown in the top half of Figure 7-2.
>
> Then study your list and try to define a proposed strategic competency that is a combination of the listed skills, processes, and knowledge. When trying to identify potential competencies, it's helpful to think of common success factors that span many areas of the business.
>
> Once you have a list of possible competencies, rate each for compliance with the definition of a strategic competency. Any that get at least two "high" ratings and no "low" ratings are current strategic competencies.

Competencies of Different Sizes

Not all companies play in the same markets. Obviously, a company such as Wal-Mart or IBM needs a really big, encompassing strategic competency to sustain itself. A smaller company can develop a very specific focus and just dominate that particular area.

Strategic Competencies

Skills, Processes, Knowledge	A	B	C	D
Design engineering skills	X			
Rapid response to customer problems		X		
Process engineering skills			X	
Empirical failure point database	X		X	
Materials expertise for internal cushioning	X		X	
CAD process/tools for rapid design of special internal packaging materials	X	X		
Processing of wide web materials			X	
Catalog layout skills				
Low-cost, high-throughput coating process			X	
Materials expertise for decorative artwork				X
Direct mail knowledge of large customer database				
Artistic design skills for external packages				X
Rapid product development process	X	X		
Know-how and relationship to turn new 3M materials into packaging solutions	X			
JIT raw material program			X	
Unique "look" with two-color embossed foil exterior designs				X

Candidate Strategic Competencies	Value to Customer	Differentiation from Competition	Difficulty to Copy
A. Interior Packaging Design Expertise	H	H	M
B. Customer Service	H	L	M
C. Cost-Effective Mfg. of Wide Web Materials	H	M	H
D. Exterior Packaging Appearance	H	H	H

Figure 7-2. Strategic competencies analysis

No Competencies? Don't Fret

After a thorough search, many companies will not find a current strategic competency. Since strategic competencies are a big deal, this is more common than you might think. Not finding one, however, is not a death sentence for your company.

Fortunately, since strategic competencies are knowledge-based assets, you can build them by enhancing your intellectual assets. Training, building experience, and hiring to fill in specific knowledge gaps in the organization are all useful techniques. But before you embark on building and enhancing competencies, you should figure out more about your strategies so as to avoid building the "wrong" competencies—competencies that would be incompatible with your strategic vision. We'll come back to this topic in Chapter 14.

Working through the last three chapters should give you a good understanding of the current situation facing your business. This context is important for sound strategic planning. Now it's time to build on that base and develop the critical assumptions that will allow you to choose your future—to craft strategy.

Tales from the Strategy Vault

American Lock manufactures solid-body padlocks. It's a much smaller market than that dominated by the more familiar Master Lock, which makes laminated locks. For most people a laminated lock is fine, but certain situations need the extra security of a solid-body padlock. American Lock has developed a focused strategic competency. Its competency is not in the design and manufacture of all locks, but just solid-body locks. The company has taken a position and dominated it, rather than trying to compete on Master Lock's turf.

Part Three

Figure Out the Way You Expect Things to Be

WHAT DO YOU THINK IS GOING TO HAPPEN IN THE FUTURE and what kind of company do you think is going to win?

In this section, you will learn about assumptions and why it's essential to have reasonable estimates about the makeup of the future. You will build consensus for a view of the business environment over the next three to five years. You will identify, develop, and screen opportunities—the lifeblood of growing companies. Of course, not everything in the future will go our way. Part of looking into the future is imagining the world as it could go spectacularly wrong. It probably won't happen, but you should consider those scenarios so that you'll be prepared if it does.

Finally, we'll get you to take a longer look into the future. First, you'll try to figure out the important trends and scenarios for your industry. Then you'll determine the characteristics of a winner in that specific future.

So turn the page, and begin to build a picture of what the future holds for you.

chapter 8

Make Assumptions About the World

THE WORLD IS CHANGING AND WE'RE ALL GOING ALONG FOR THE RIDE. The changes that are coming are unknown, of course, and our lives and our success will depend on what the future holds. When planning, some will guess at the future, while others will just pretend that there are no changes coming. It's up to you. Some will be ready for the changes, but most will probably be surprised. If they're lucky, it will be a pleasant surprise. But we all know that everybody gets lucky once in a while and nobody gets lucky all of the time. But still, no matter how you approach the future, it's inevitable—changes are coming.

So what are you going to do about the future? As you might guess, we recommend taking some time to think about the coming changes. Make some assumptions. You may be surprised at where it can all lead. Here's a hint: success.

Why Assume?

When the sun comes up in the morning, it doesn't surprise us. We assume it will happen. Knowing what the sun will do takes a bit of educated guess-work (knowing a few physical laws) and a lot of simple instinct. Because the sun has been rising for generations, you don't really even have to think about it. That's just how it is.

Some business situations are as simple as the rhythm of sun. Others are more complex. The things that affect sunrises of business can be weird, unpredictable stuff that you can't possibly guess about without a bit of study and research. If it can be so difficult, why bother? Why assume? Because there's a future. Good assumptions are necessary for a good plan. Although no one can totally and accurately predict the future, it's also impossible to do planning without making some hypotheses about future events.

> **Strategic Tip**
>
> Assumptions are temporary estimates about some probable future event or development over which you have no particular control. Assumptions lie at the heart of all strategic plans. Assumptions should be treated very differently from facts. Be careful not to confuse the two.

Strategy is about planning for the future. If the world would stay the same, you could just plan once and then forget about it. But the world is always changing, so decisions that make sense today may not make sense in the future. You need to sit down and spend some thoughtful time considering what the changes will be, how they will affect your business, and how they will affect the critical decisions that you need to make for your business for the considerable future. Based on what you expect, what are you going to do?

If you don't have any expectations, you probably don't have a very good strategy for the changes that are coming. If you've been thoughtful and figured that things are somehow going to shift to the left or to the right, you can be ready for that shift. The key is to be thoughtful. There's a difference between making an educated guess and just throwing a dart. If you blindly guess and simply say, "Um, well, we'll guess whatever," you can run into a lot of trouble.

In business, you have to make decisions based on how you *assume* the world is going to change. If you don't, you *assume* (by default) that the world is going to stay the same. If you decide that you're simply not going to decide, you run the risk of being blind-sided by change.

How to Assume

Give thoughtful consideration to the key drivers. Thoughtful consideration takes the important factors under advisement. When you're trying to figure out the future, your business will have certain drivers that are important. Figuring those out is the first step toward reaching a set of assumptions that can help you define a strategy.

The future you face is composed of a number of small pieces. Your job in reaching a set of assumptions is to put them all together to form a clear picture of the future as you expect it.

You're looking for underpinnings, the stuff under the stuff that drives your business. Suppose you're looking at profit levels. Well, there might be an influence from the competition. If there are more competitors, prices tend to go down; if there are fewer competitors, prices tend to go up. The goal is to increase profits, so part of what you're trying to figure out is whether there will be more or fewer competitors in the market. If you examine this assumption closely, you will look at barriers to entry in the market, because that would affect how many companies are in it. There may be other factors that influence market entry as well—such things as government regulation, capital requirements, and technology.

Understanding the underlying causes for changes in your assumptions is like peeling an onion—there always seems to be another layer underneath. As you peel back the layers of the onion, you get into increasingly refined areas. You don't need to go down to every level, but instinct should tell you how far to go in order to understand. When you consider the richness of facts that you understand and you put them in a logical setting, you form a complex

Tales from the Strategy Vault

Ostriches, like some businesses, hide from fear of the unknown by sticking their heads in the sand. This doesn't solve their problems and leaves them exposed as easy prey.

notion of how you expect the future to be. Although things may not always turn out exactly the way you expect, you will know enough to go forward with confidence.

Of course, you have to draw the line somewhere or you could be trying to figure out the smallest details. Once again, we recommend instinct. Let your people think. Don't get obsessed with perfection or every little blip and hiccup. You want the big picture.

That big picture includes different circumstances. For instance, think about what it takes to build a skyscraper in Iowa versus what it takes to build a skyscraper in San Francisco. What would your assumptions be and how would they differ for each location?

Avoid Wishful Thinking

One of the easiest mistakes when making strategic assumptions is wishful thinking. We've all seen it. Rather than confront reality, we construct an assumption that supports the way we want things to be: sales forecasts that project unrealistic growth, operations plans that show unprecedented efficiency gains, cash flow projections that assume that all customers pay in 30 days, and so on.

When exploring a new opportunity, managers in many companies assume that the competitors will roll over and allow a new entry into the market. When asked what they themselves would do if confronted with a new entrant, they cite all sorts of nasty things they would do to repel the attack. Only then do they realize that they're guilty of wishful thinking when they assume anything less than a vigorous response from competitors.

You'll be making decisions about the future of your business based on your assumptions. Don't let wishful thinking lead you to make a plan for a future that won't be there when you arrive.

Don't Put Too Much Stock in Assumptions

You cannot hold your assumptions as facts. That's a trap a lot of companies fall into where they begin to treat an assumption as if it were reality. The future is the only test of an assumption. You need to be able to maneuver around inside of your assumptions and even to jump outside of them if conditions change enough to make your assumptions irrelevant.

Of course, some people have enough experience to simply state an assumption as if it were fact and have enough credibility for others with less experience to simply accept the assumption as reality. For instance, someone could say something like, "Hey, I've been in this business for 40 years, and I know that *every* time we get a cool, rainy winter, beef prices go up." And maybe that person really has good intuition. That's knowledge that other companies may not have, and

Tales from the Strategy Vault

We know of a company that invested heavily in a new product, expecting to make great margins. Unfortunately, the margin expectations were based on the pricing of a competitor that was already selling this product. When the new product entered the market, the competitor cut the prices on its product dramatically. This price cut nearly eliminated profits for the new product for several years. Yes, there was fat in the existing pricing in the market when the company evaluated the opportunity, but there was also a competitor that was willing and able to defend its turf. Assuming that this competitor would not or could not defend this market was wishful thinking that turned out to be very costly.

it should be built into your process of developing assumptions. But nobody should ever be considered to be above question and scrutiny. An assumption is something that may be true or not true; treat it that way.

Many companies we've worked with have venerable managers on their teams with plenty of valuable experience in their business. Unfortunately, experience often causes some tendency to make assumption errors.

The managers of one manufacturer, for example, felt the only way they could continue to compete was as a commodity player, because a very senior manager with 20 years at the company had tremendous experience building the company by lowballing bids for contract work.

This was a $50 million company that was about to hit the wall with this strategy for two reasons:

- There was tremendous competition from Asian manufacturers whose quality was low, but improving.
- Large domestic competitors had invested heavily in automation, which gave them a big cost advantage on long run jobs with fairly high quality levels.

Basically, the past strategy of this company—being cheap because it was small—was about to become irrelevant. This didn't prevent the senior manager from pushing his vision, which was to continue with the old strategy. It made sense from his perspective: he knew how to work the old strategy, it seemed more stable, and his instincts told him it would work because it had worked in the past. His experience gave him such credibility with the other managers that, even though they understood the need for change in their strategy, they didn't switch away from the old strategy until three years later, when their sales had dropped by 20%.

Avoid Naive Projections

The simplest assumption is to project that past trends will continue indefinitely into the future. This is what statisticians call a "naive projection" because it places blind faith in continuation of past trends, rather than giving thoughtful weight to each of the factors that make up a trend.

Trends are relatively easy to follow, but what you want to find most of all are turning points in a trend. There's where the greatest opportunities lie. If you can be realistic about the world and the way it is and will be, rather than the way you wish it would be, you can anticipate those key turning points in time to profit from them.

For instance, the long-established stability in the supply and demand of oil led people to have rather naive projections about the price of oil in the early 1970s. And then suddenly things changed and those assumptions were absolutely backwards from reality. Who could have imagined that all of these small countries would have the gumption to get together and raise the prices? Gosh. Well, any number of people could have imagined it if they had just thought about the conditions of the world just prior to the first OPEC gatherings.

The examples abound. Think about how people thought about the cost of health care as a fixed expense until suddenly the cost became a big concern for everyone. And prior to the 1990s, people held strong to the belief that the economy goes up and down, but yet there has been a historic period of sustained growth.

Remember: things change—even if it means that they stay the same for longer than usual. That's a change. The question is, when did "longer than usual" start?

Turning points are easy to identify in hindsight, but you need to figure a way to find them ahead of time. And for those that defy reasonable prediction, you need to know the range of possible scenarios—to be ready for whichever of them actually happens. You do this by making assumptions and reassessing them frequently to allow you to adapt to ever-changing conditions.

Formulating good assumptions is not hard, but it takes practice. Collecting the wisdom of several people is the best approach, rather than making "lone ranger" predictions. It's truly a skill that a management team can build over time. Identify the critical factors, apply your best judgment, and see how it all turns out. Whether it be good or not so perfect, you'll learn from the experience. With a consistent effort, your results will improve, and before long others will be amazed at the savvy of your team.

Beware of Nasty Surprises

Try as you may, things won't always turn out as you expect: there will be surprises. Some will be pleasant surprises, strokes of good luck. But some may be "nasty surprises," the result of either adverse, uncontrollable events or a serious systematic assumption error. There's little we can do to influence the uncontrollable course of events, but we can take precautions to minimize some common assumption errors.

Minimize Assumption Errors

When you hear of a company that got into big trouble with its strategy, the cause can usually be traced back to some significant assumption error. It can get really bad. Here are two classic examples:

- IBM made an assumption error in the 1970s and 1980s when it assumed that its model for bringing computers to corporate America was right. Basically, IBM believed that all systems needed to be under the centralized control of some information systems (IS) professional. That's because IBM's customer contacts were IS professionals who had a vested interest in the status quo. So did IBM. Unfortunately for IBM, there were many others who did not have such an interest and they turned to smaller, entrepreneurial companies for desktop computers.

■ Xerox made assumption errors based on listening to its customers—technical people in backroom print shops of companies. All of these people claimed to need bigger and better machines to be able to handle the variety of jobs that came their way. So Xerox kept making machines with more and more bells and whistles, while Canon came in and captured the emerging personal photocopier market.

Although we cannot eliminate all assumption errors, there are four steps that will greatly reduce them.

The Four Steps to Minimizing Assumption Errors

1. Recognize that all assumptions are temporary estimates. You have to take possibilities into account and recognize that you need to build flexibility into your plan. Understanding these are temporary assumptions helps you build some escape paths—alternatives to your strategy so that you don't stake your future on one single thing with no way out.
2. You must be careful to separate assumptions from facts. Many CEOs and others with long experience have pet theories that they like to treat as facts. After a while, they begin to think that their predictions aren't assumptions but truth. It needs to be clear that some things are assumptions and some are facts. We stress that you be eagle-eyed to spot assumptions posing as facts.
3. Lay out multiple scenarios so you know what to do in the most likely cases and also what to do in a worst-case scenario. Scenario planning sensitizes you to the range of possibilities and keeps you alert to whichever scenario is developing.
4. Review all assumptions frequently, at least once a quarter. Change drives planning and every time the world changes—which can happen quite frequently in some industries—you need to think about replanning. For instance, Internet companies probably need to recalibrate their assumptions at least as often as every couple of months. Not that long ago there were companies that didn't have to update their assumptions more than once every five or 10 years. But change is infiltrating all of business now. And making assumptions is a key skill in strategic planning.

Minimizing assumption errors reduces the probability of nasty surprises and, conversely, leaves you prepared to take advantage of the pleasant surprises.

Serendipity Happens to the Prepared Company

Louis Pasteur once said, "Chance favors only a prepared mind." It may often seem to the world like people just stumble into lucky situations, but the truth is that people often get into lucky situations by design. Sure, it's good to be lucky. But the accidental invention or discovery is really the result of someone who was prepared to take advantage of an unexpected result.

In some ways, creating a strategy in business is like going on a family trip. Think about the preparations you take before a trip. You pull out a map to make assumptions about what's out there. You think about alternate routes, about the weather, and about whether to pack a lunch or plan to stop somewhere. You think about alternatives and possibilities. Maybe your car doesn't get good gas mileage, so you don't want to take the route that has only two gas stations. You want to take the Interstate with its regular rest areas. If you think ahead of time, it may appear to others who left at the same time as you that you picked the right route just by luck. But it wasn't luck.

It's the same in business. For instance, Nike can be perceived as simply lucky enough to sign Michael Jordan at the right time in his career and then ride on the tails of his extraordinary talents. But a company such as Nike is in the business of signing athletes to promote its products. Nike didn't get lucky. Nike did what it set out to do—find and sign the right athlete.

So how do you prepare for the unexpected? The first step is to try to identify major discontinuities—the big things that will change in your industry, your markets, your customers, or your supplier base. The idea is to stretch your thinking into the future. Remember that there's stuff way out there, science fiction-type stuff, but in your strategic planning you need to spend some time thinking: Will you be prepared if the ball gets knocked your way? Will you have enough flexibility built in so you can take advantage of luck?

Assumptions are a critical element of any strategic plan. You need to understand how they differ from facts and how to handle them to ensure that you develop them properly to minimize the common pitfalls. In the next chapter you will apply these concepts to develop assumptions about your business environment, opportunities, threats, and more.

chapter 9

Make Assumptions About the Business Environment

ALWAYS REMEMBER THAT NO MATTER HOW BIG YOUR SHIP, it is still in the ocean. By that we mean that there are forces out there that impact your business. Your business functions in a dynamic, huge—yes, even global—ocean and there are waves that roll through that ocean. Some waves are bigger than others and some you don't see coming. But most of them you'll see if you look. That's the key. You have to look.

The business environment is a set of specific factors that will likely change to some degree over time. These changes will affect your operations and your results. The things that affect your business will affect other businesses as well. Think of the business environment as weather. Maybe it will change today, or maybe tomorrow. Perhaps it won't change until the next day or the day after that, but you know as sure as the sun will rise that at some time, even if you live in a relatively stable climate, it will change—because there's no such thing as a perfectly stable climate.

So what do you think is going to happen? Is it going to rain, or snow, or be sunnier than ever before? Are competitors going to invest in new technology? Will there be a great new technology out there that everybody needs? Is one of your suppliers going to raise prices? Is your market is going to expand or contract? Is there some new law on the horizon that could change your industry? What do you think? If you examine the specific factors one at a time, you can begin to paint a picture of the future.

Assumptions for Market Segments

In Chapter 4, you segmented your existing business into about six to eight market segments, and you analyzed the current situation for each. Now you need to figure out what is going to happen to them *in the future*. You want to examine each market segment and make assumptions about them in some detail.

> ### Strategic Tip
>
> Use a three- to five-year horizon for your assumptions—depending on the rate of change in your industry. For some fast-growth industries, a five-year time horizon is so fuzzy that it isn't worth much, while others may find they need to look a little beyond five years. In most industries, though, making assumptions three to five years down the road is reasonable.

Examine the earlier questions about market segments all over again—this time with an eye on the future. And now there are new questions to examine because you're looking three to five years down the road.

Four Critical Market Segment Assumptions

Remember that, in the beginning of this process, you identified market segments that represented distinct groups of buying behaviors. There are two strategically important questions:

- What is going to happen to those segments?
- What will make things change?

There are four specific things to examine:

- needs and preferences
- growth rate
- profit levels
- what might wipe out the market altogether.

Needs and Preferences

When you look at *needs*, you're trying to anticipate how the customer's needs will change over the next five years. One good way to figure out the needs of the future is to take a look at the preferences of today. Often, things that are preferred now will become needs in the future.

However, this is not the only way that needs arise. Sometimes, a small, but specific need arises from the application of technology in meeting a substantial, enduring need. For example, the need for transportation has existed throughout human history, but in the past hundred years it has been met through the use of internal combustion vehicles—automobiles. This technology has created a need for fuel that will abate only if the broader need—transportation—can be met without fuel.

When you're trying to figure future *preferences*, it helps to look at trends in society. The fact that people are becoming more environmentally conscious could be a trend that may mean something in your industry. Or the fact that people are becoming more electronically interconnected could lead to many changes in preferences. Often people don't know that they prefer something until it's available.

Growth Rate

Is this market segment going to grow? If so, by how much? Not just for you, but for all competitors in the market. When you try to anticipate the growth rate, you need to think about the drivers that could send the market segment up or down. What are the drivers that will create opportunities and what are the drivers that will create threats to the whole market? You want to try to identify them. What are the things that will be good for the whole market—for you *and* for your competitors?

Some of the drivers will be immediately apparent, while others may not occur to you until you peer deeper into your customers' lives. For instance, if you sell tires, anything that would cause people to drive more and therefore need to buy more tires would be a positive driver in your market and anything that would make people want to drive less would be a negative driver. So, cheap gasoline and anything that would cause people to buy more automobiles, such as an expanding economy, would be positive drivers in the tire business.

Figuring out good assumptions for future growth rates takes careful thought on several levels. Sometimes you have to dig down a layer or two to find the real drivers for your industry.

Profit Levels

Can you make money in this market segment? The idea is not to simply survive but to make a profit. So, just as you did with growth rate, you also want consider the positive and negative drivers that affect profitability in the industry. How much money is there to be made in the next three to five years?

For instance, if you're in an industry that's consolidating so that there are likely to be fewer players in a market, then the remaining players may be more profitable. Each competitor can get a bigger chunk of sales without head-to-head competition and there probably won't be as much price-cutting, because each company can take a specific part of the market. The competitors will likely still fight for market share, but the struggle will probably be less intense and so profits should be higher. Understanding the direction of profit levels in a market segment is a key part of strategy.

What Might Wipe Out the Market Altogether

Free markets are like a jungle. There are predatory ideas that surface every day in the world. Sometimes these ideas can quickly destroy an industry that seemed as stable as a rock. This may happen because the need served by the industry just disappears or—far more likely—because someone comes up with a far better way to serve a need *with an entirely different product or service*.

The latter situation is called *displacement*. A need may be served by completely different means over time. For instance, in the old days, the only way to make copies of a letter was to use carbon paper when you typed the letter. Various improvements, such as mimeography, were invented, but they all had drawbacks, so carbon paper remained widely used. Then, one day someone invented xerography, virtually eliminating the biggest need for carbon paper. As another example, think about how the print industry has been changed by the laser printer. For many low-volume uses, a good laser printer is now better than a million-dollar printing press.

Markets can also be displaced by changes in the business environment. When the government regulated the delivery of mail in the mid-19th century, making it illegal to compete with the post office, delivery companies like Wells Fargo saw a significant part of their business disappear overnight. The Pony Express has been replaced by trains, trucks, and planes. These technologies made the U.S. Postal Service an efficient provider of basic postal service through most of this century. Recent changes in technology—some of them in the area of management—have caused bits of this market to splinter off, even though the USPS had a clear monopoly. The USPS was supplanted by UPS in package shipping, then by Federal Express in overnight delivery, and lately by electronic mail in the basic letter business.

> **Strategic Tip**
>
> The introduction of foreign competition in almost any industry will change the dynamics dramatically. Prior to the 1970s, the American automobile industry was absolutely dominated by the American companies. Now, driving down an American highway is like driving through a melting pot of global manufacturing.

These examples should be enough of a warning. It's possible. Things may come along that can wipe out the reason your company exists.

The worksheet in Figure 9-1 will help you get a handle on your assumptions for your market segments.

At this time we do not foresee developments in candy technology that would eliminate the requirement for protection from crushing. To our knowledge, no such research is underway.

> **Outside the Meeting**
>
> The worksheet in Figure 9-1 should be prepared following the first and prior to the second meeting. One page should be done for *each* market segment. This is the second page that analyzes a market segment; it should be assigned to the same individuals who prepared the information for the worksheet in Figure 4-3.

Assumptions About Competition

What is the strategy of your *competitors*? What could affect their strategy? You know who we are talking about—those people, that other company that wants to earn the same dollars that you have your sights on. How do they think they're going to get there and, more important, would you have a way to beat them if you knew their strategy?

Are your competitors growing or shrinking? Are they going to be looking to do work with one type of customer or with another? Are they going to be

Date:_____
ASSUMPTIONS FOR MARKET SEGMENT   Worksheet No.: 4.1-1
Originators:_____

Segment Designation: *Interior Packaging for Hard Candy*		
Future Changes in Market Needs: At this time we do not foresee developments in candy technology that would eliminate requirement for protection from crushing. To our knowledge, no such research is underway.		
Future Changes in Market Preferences: Three-day delivery.		
Threats to Market (Factors that might cause size of *total market* **defined on Worksheet 1.1 to shrink)**	**Probability** **L, M, H**	**Impact** **L, M, H**
1. Hard candies lose appeal because of cost.	M	M
2. Hard candies lose appeal because of change in taste.	L	M
3. Substantial price reductions from building excess capacity.	M-H	M
Opportunities for Market (Factors that might cause size of *total market* **defined on Worksheet 1.1 to grow)**		
1. New candy products that increase overall candy sales.	L	L
Rate of Future Real Industry Market Growth (What is the expected change in size of *total market* **as defined on corresponding Worksheet 1.1?)** Will grow by 3% per year over next few years.		
Average Future Industry Profit Level (What is the expected profit level for the *total market* **as defined on corresponding Worksheet 1.1?)** 38% contribution margin and 11% Return on Invested Capital (ROIC)		
Future Potential for Product/Service Displacement: None likely.		
Other Significant Future Events: We do not foresee any other significant future events.		

Figure 9-1. Assumptions for market segment

looking to sell to customers based on service? On technology? Quality? You want to take all of this into account because a battle against a competitor is a bit like a fencing match. You want to be where they're not thrusting and to thrust where they are. Ideally, you do not want to go head to head with anyone: that's a recipe for failure. If they're selling on price, perhaps you should sell on quality.

When you make assumptions about your competition, you want to devise a way to take advantage of what you know. So what do you know about your competitors? Try writing something about their strategy in a couple of sentences.

You also want to cover the things that could happen in your industry that could upset the balance of power. For instance, will there be changes in distribution channels that could favor one business model over another? Will there be changes in capacities? Is some company bringing new capacity on line? That certainly may affect that particular company, but it will also affect the whole industry.

Finally, you just want to know how you're going to stack up against competitors in the future. Will your strengths stand up against their strengths and, more important, have you figured a way to put your strengths against their weaknesses? Take a hard look at the important stuff in your industry and see if you think you'll improve more than your competition. Both of you will improve. Will you be better? By how much?

List your company and major competitors in the market segment

> **Tales from the Strategy Vault**
>
> Superior Telecom makes copper wire and cable for the telephone industry. It would seem at first that this company would be at a distinct disadvantage, since so much of the world is being converted to fiber optic cable. But this company recognized what much of the world failed to understand—that copper is still the most cost-effective medium for serving the "last mile" of the network, from the central office to the home. While the main trunk lines are going to fiber optic cables, very few of the thousands of communities are running fiber into homes. People are still predicting that will come at some point, but for now the company that still makes copper cable is doing quite well, despite the trend. This company has more than quadrupled its worth in a short time because it understood the flip side of a trend that many of its competitors were following.

under examination in a table like that shown at the bottom of Figure 9-2, using a simple rating scheme: '+,' 'OK,' and '-.' You can use '++' and '- -' ratings sparingly for extreme performance. Figure 9-3, a normal distribution can help you see where you stand on the average in your industry.

Rate each competitor in several categories that typically affect competitive position. Identify those that are typical, or average in their ability to meet the needs and preferences of the market segment. If there are some that are substantially better or worse, rate these '+' or '-.' Take a similar approach with each of the other categories.

Rating some of these categories requires careful attention:

Cost. Don't be fooled by a company's price point; we're talking cost here. Price can be anywhere depending on what margin the company is willing to accept. Focus on factors that give a true cost advantage (e.g., material cost, wage rates, overhead, process technology).

Date: _____
Worksheet No.: 4.2
Originators: _____

COMPETITION ASSUMPTIONS FOR MARKET SEGMENT

Segment Designation: *Interior Packaging for Hard Candy*

Competitors' Future Strategic Moves:
1. Brown is working hard on product development. Something (unspecified) is likely to be developed.
2. ABC will probably establish a plant on the West Coast.
3. National will probably continue to diversify.
4. XYZ will establish its own distributors.
5. Federal will probably not survive.

Other Significant Future Developments:
1. Brown will continue to build capacity and reputation.
2. ABC may experience cost difficulties in their expansion unless they obtain equity financing (which is doubtful).
3. Although industry volume will grow at a 3% annual rate over the next few years, capacity will be added at an even faster rate. Capacity utilization will be down to 75% within two years.
4. Industry profits will average 11% (ROIC) over next 3-5 years, barring unexpected major economic developments.

Competitive Position and Future Market Share	Us	Brown	ABC	XYZ	National
Ability to Meet Market Needs and Preferences	++	+	OK	OK	–
Quality	+	+	OK	OK	–
Costs (not price)	OK	+	OK	OK	OK
Service	++	+	OK	OK	–
Reputation	++	+	OK	OK	–
Financial Strength	OK	+	OK	OK	–
Proprietary Position	OK	OK	OK	OK	–
Current Market Share	24%	33%	10%	10%	10%
Future Market Share	30%	33%	9%	12%	13%

Figure 9-2. Analyzing how you stack up versus competitors

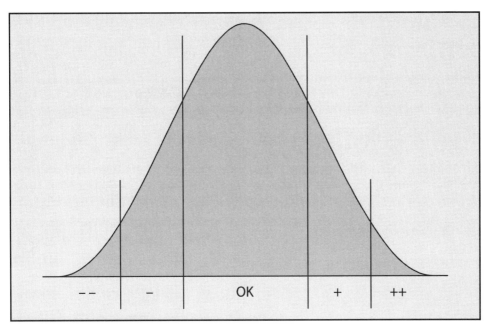

Figure 9-3. Figuring out where you stand

Financial Strength. This category refers to the financial muscle a company has to pursue opportunities in a market. Strong cash flows and wealthy owners are often more indicative of strength than debt-free balance sheets.

Proprietary Position. This category certainly includes legally protected stuff like patents and trademarks. But you should also consider anything a

> ### Strategic Tip
> As much as possible, ensure that competitive position is rated relative to the other companies listed and the distribution centered about 'OK.' Any horizontal row in Worksheet 4.2 should average out to be 'OK.' If every company has 'good' quality, then they should all be 'OK,' not all '+.'

company has that others can't get or duplicate in three to five years by just throwing money at it (e.g., real estate location, key talent who are owners of the company).

The worksheet shown in Figure 9-4 (page 111) will help you get a handle on your assumptions about your competitors in each market segment.

Assumptions About the Business Environment

Your world will change in ways that you can not control, and you will have to react to those changes. The best that you can do is put together a set of assumptions about what you think is going to happen in four specific areas: Supplier Markets, Technology, Economy, and Government Regulation. We covered those in great detail in Chapter 5. Now it's time to think about what's coming.

Every company needs to consider each of these areas and formulate specific assumptions. What will technology look like in three years? What will be the impact of e-commerce? Will states be able to levy sales tax on electronic commerce? Where do you see regulations going that are specific to your industry? You need to look at all of these things, but focus only on those things that will have a significant impact on your business.

It's important to write these assumptions down so that all can review them and agree or disagree. Lack of consensus about the future is one of the biggest factors that slow strategic decisions to a crawl.

Assumptions about the business environment help you along the way toward developing a cohesive strategy. They lead you to understand how you think the world will be. And then, you can start figuring out what opportunities to chase in order to win in that world.

> **Outside the Meeting**
>
> The worksheet in Figure 9-4 should be done following the first and prior to the second meeting. One page should be done for *each* market segment. This is the third page that analyzes a market segment; it should be assigned to the same individuals who prepared the information for the worksheets in Figures 4-3 and 9-1.

Will our suppliers raise their prices? Will

> **Strategic Tip**
>
> Keep your responses brief. If you can say it in a sentence, don't take a paragraph. If you can say it in a phrase, don't take a sentence. If you can say it in a word, do it. No one will take the time to reread pages of analysis, but they will reread a bullet point or two.

> **Outside the Meeting**
>
> Take time to write down your assumptions in each of these key areas. This should be done following the first and prior to the second meeting. It is usually assigned to the same individuals who prepared the information for Figures 5-2 through 5-5.

OTHER IMPORTANT ASSUMPTIONS   Date:_____
Worksheet No.: 4.3

Future Changes in Technology:
- Our semi-automatic machine for mid-size work will be successful in terms of effectiveness and efficiency. It will be completed within two years and will give us a substantial cost advantage in this area. (90% probability)
- ABC and National, as well as ourselves, will have great difficulty with the development of large-scale capability. Chances for success are probably no better than 1 in 10, and in no case would it occur before five years.
- No other changes are expected, but there is always the possibility that something unexpected could happen.

Future Changes in Supplier Markets:
Next year we will see the following in our raw material market:
1. Volume will be 13.4MM-14.6MM tons. Most likely 14MM.
2. Capacity will be 15.4MM tons. (99.9% probability)
3. Capacity utilization will fall from 83% to 75%, causing softer pricing.

Future Changes in Economy:
1. Constant-dollar GDP will continue to rise moderately (3-4%). There will be no recession. (95% probability)
2. Industrial production will continue to expand as capacity expands. (80% probability)
3. Investment will rise by 4%. (75% probability)
4. Consumer spending will rise by 4%. (60% probability)
5. Employment will rise, and unemployment will hold steady at around 5.3%. (80% probability)
6. The CPI will rise by 6%. (90% probability)
7. The PPI will rise by 5%. (90% probability)

These assumptions depend on moderately restrictive Federal Reserve policy through next year and no unexpected shocks to the economy.

Future Changes in Government Regulations:
Both major political parties will continue to move to the right in response to the popular move in that direction. Radical movement is not expected. In general, we expect moderate relaxation in government regulation and continuation of moderate efforts to reduce welfare and the deficit.

Figure 9-4. Planning assumptions

chapter 10

Make Assumptions About Threats and Opportunities

I T'S TIME FOR SOME FUN. Strategy, even the simplified kind, involves a lot of work to get the information necessary for informed decisions. Once you've got it, you get to start figuring what's next. So, in the course of this book you've gathered all of that stuff and you have your foundation. Now it's time to dream, time to expand your thoughts about your future.

The world of the future will bring changes. When strategizing, you need to figure out how to take advantage of those changes and how to avoid being hurt by them. Some of these changes will be opportunities and some will be threats. You need to deal with both, but you must be sure that in creating your strategy you focus on opportunities. No company has ever become great solely because it dealt with all of its threats. You become great by turning opportunity into success.

It's fun to turn on your creative juices. It's where you lay the groundwork for strong results. Sure, you need to take care of managing what's happening today and you certainly need to be aware of threats that may arise, but your future depends on how you set yourself up. So, what do you have in mind?

First, Let's Avoid Extinction

Not only are opportunities fun and exciting, but pursuing them is essential to survival. No one likes to talk about it, but companies die. How many? Well, about a third of the *Fortune* 500 have vanished since the first list was produced in 1955. These are big companies; for smaller companies the survival rate is even lower.

It's doubtful that the managers of any of these companies planned to fail. Like the dinosaurs of ancient times, most of them just didn't see it coming in time. Many were successful, even dominant. In fact, it's often success that blinds a company to the impending change. Cries of "Don't tinker with success!" or "That toy product can't touch us!" echo off boardroom walls—and now a PC maker, Compaq Computer, owns the once dominant mini-computer company, Digital Equipment Corporation. Other companies, like Pan Am Airlines, got surprised by aggressive competition and tried to cut costs and 'downsize' themselves into success, but that just left them with fewer resources and fewer options. Times, tastes, and needs change.

Like a species, if a company is going to survive in a competitive environment it needs a few mutations that will allow it to adapt to new conditions. It needs to consider, explore, and act on opportunities. In a proactive company, one with a plan, the threats in a changing environment become the seeds of great new opportunities to eclipse past accomplishments. So let's generate some good opportunities.

> **Strategic Tip**
>
> "Denominator management," where a company tries to prop up its return on investment by focusing on reducing assets rather than increasing profits through innovation and healthy revenue generation, is seldom a long-term course to success.

$$ROI = \frac{Profits}{Investment}$$

Brainstorming as an Art Form

Good ideas make wealth. There's nothing better than a good idea. But not all ideas are good. Many can, in fact, be downright bad. A creative process like brainstorming works best when it is unbounded, free to consider anything—even the outlandish. Sometimes, the most ridiculous ideas can turn out to be the best... and sometimes not. But you don't want to miss anything because it could be *that thing*.

Creativity and innovation are not sideshows to business—they are a central and critical means of driving profitability. Many companies, however, discourage real outside-the-box thinking. The culture is such that people try to think only with their 'smart brain cells,' suppressing ideas they think won't be heartily embraced by the CEO or peers on the planning team. The result is the dreaded 'group think.' Though allowing nonconformity sometimes takes a little longer, it must be tolerated in order to ensure there are a few good ideas in the sea of run-of-the-mill ideas.

> **Tales from the Strategy Vault**
>
> Most great innovators, like Thomas Edison, have more bad ideas than good. When asked if he was depressed about having tested 10,000 materials for light bulb filaments without success, Edison replied, "Heavens no, that *is* success! I now know 10,000 things that don't work." You have to take the time to generate many ideas and to sift through all of them, at least in a cursory fashion, if you hope to find the seed that can spawn a company like General Electric.

Don't start with the old list; it won't work. The idea of brainstorming is to take what could turn into an open-ended discussion of old ideas and turn it into something useful and productive—a creative and vibrant interchange in which managers play off each other's ideas to aim for something new. Make sure you encourage the free flow of ideas with no criticism. You want people to take the dare and put their idea up for consideration, even if it may seem a bit off the wall.

> **Tales from the Strategy Vault**
>
> Use your "stupid" brain cells when you brainstorm. Most managers are taught to only use their "smart" brain cells—the ones with common sense—and to leave the "stupid" ones at home. Well, in brainstorming, you want unusual, creative, and even silly ideas. In brainstorming, "stupid" ideas are good as long as they have creative juice.

One of the things that you usually find in brainstorming is that in the first five or 10 minutes, you get a dump of ideas that are the tried and true. They may be good ideas, but they've probably been around a while. So far, nothing new. Then there's usually a lull, a sudden stop to the flow.

In this lull the leader is a key player. The leader must power the group through the lull, peppering the team with questions and ideas to force people to keep thinking. When you reach the lull, you're getting closer to the magic. The leader, through analogy and creative questioning, must try and draw people out to think new, creative thoughts. It's often the second wave of ideas following the lull that are the most exciting. Each idea spawns another new thought and, if well orchestrated, they build to a crescendo that takes the team into new territory.

So how do you stimulate creative thinking about opportunities? Well, take ideas that are already stimulating, and then push beyond those with more questions.

For instance, we've worked earlier with strategic competencies (Chapter 7). Look at these and ask:

- Where can our strategic competencies lead us?
- If we increased one strategic competency by a factor of 10, where could that lead us?
- What other industries might value our strategic competencies?

> ### Tales from the Strategy Vault
>
> One of the authors is a big fan of the Walt Disney Company, often even wearing Mickey Mouse business shirts when he works with companies. At one meeting with a manufacturer of bicycle helmets, someone in the brainstorming session suggested it would be cool if they could get Mickey Mouse on a helmet. Someone else suggested that the hot children's toy at the time was Teenage Mutant Ninja Turtles. They followed this 'dumb' idea all the way through to licensing the product—and in one year this $5 million company sold $15 million worth of this one new product, Ninja Turtle helmets. Dumb ideas are worth taking a step further.

But don't stop there. Examine everything to search for new opportunities:

- What new products can we develop?
- What new markets can we pursue?
- What internal operating improvements can we pursue?
- How can we make our strengths work more for us?

Take what you think is going to happen and make it an opportunity:

- Who will do great in that environment?

And there's always room for the outrageous questions:

- How can we get our customers to think that the best thing in the world they can do is to pay us twice as much for doing what we do today?
- How can we create a situation in which our customers are always looking to bring us more business?
- How can we put ourselves out of business?
- How could we improve our value proposition by a factor of 10?

Just keep going and pushing as long as the creative level is high. Make a big list and follow ideas with more ideas. Pursue things. Don't be shy. Dream the big dream.

Evaluating the Ideas

The next step is to filter it down. The best filter in world is your brain, because when you're dealing in assumptions everything hinges on what's in your head. What do you think is going to happen? What do others in your company think? Can you all make this idea work?

Once you get past the phase of generating ideas, you enter the new phase—narrowing them down. Think about it: the last thing in the world you want to do is do extensive research on 40 or 50 items, when you'll be able to do only a half dozen at most anyway.

So you need a series of ever-finer screens. You cut the ideas one level at a time, taking more time with the surviving opportunities at each screening level and applying more and more scrutiny to them. Eventually, the short list of survivors may be subjected to something as rigorous as developing a full business case to test the merit of each.

The Initial Screen: Level 1

Immediately following the brainstorming activity, the first scan will show the silly ideas. Although they may have led to great ideas, they're be vulnerable to a quick, no-discussion cut. For instance, *Paint the building red* may have led to a great idea about promoting your logo, but the idea itself can be cut without any pain. Who really needs a red building? It's good stimulus, but it's ridiculous to start rating the idea. So what's the next idea?

> **Strategic Tip**
>
> When screening opportunities, give an idea the benefit of the doubt. If a team member is passionate about an idea, though many others may want to cut it, allow the idea to survive to the next round as long as someone will take responsibility to develop new information to help evaluate the opportunity.

The Filter: Level 2

After the obviously weak ideas have been cut, it's time to go back around to the ideas that are still alive for a bit of scrutiny. Three or four minutes should do it. The same group that did the brainstorming acts as the filter. Now, take another walk through the ideas, making a reasonable and reasoned assessment of what is feasible.

The best way to assess an opportunity is to rate it using a few criteria and a simple rating system.

We recommend you look at four things and rate them for each opportunity:

- **Perceived Value:** Rate it from 1 (very low) to 10 (very high).
- **Assumed Probability of Success:** Rate it from 0% to 100% (in 10% increments).
- **Anticipated Management Effort**: High, Moderate, or Low works best.
- **Perceived Down-Side Risk:** Use High, Moderate, or Low.

When rating *value*, you should assume (for now) that the idea will be successful. (The probability rating will address the potential that it may not be a complete success.) To rate value on the 10-point scale, consider the total return of the opportunity over its expected life less the investment cost. '10' is considered the highest value—something that transforms the business. The middle of the range (4-6) is for good contributions to the bottom line and the low end of the range for minor contributions.

> ### Strategic Tip
>
> You don't need a terribly sophisticated system. High, Medium, and Low will usually suffice. Sometimes a 1-to-10 scale works better. Don't get too quantitative: that's a good way to turn a 10-minute, potentially exciting discussion into two days of torturous bean counting ("It's got to be 87!" "No, I insist the rating be 90 out of 100!" "No, I can't go above 87!"). We recommend you avoid this sort of numeric nitpicking and recognize that both team members are agreeing on a 'High' rating.

The *probability of success* is where you factor in all things that may prevent reaching the full perceived value. Ask your team, "What is the probability that we will achieve the rating that we gave this idea for value?" 50% indicates complete uncertainty. The more you're sure an idea will or will not achieve the perceived value, the higher or lower the percentage for rating probability.

Rate the *management effort* by considering the impact that pursuing the opportunity will have on the full management team. Opportunities that have a heavy impact on one manager should be rated lower than those that have significant impact on the several top managers.

> **In the Meeting**
>
> During the first planning meeting, brainstorm new opportunities for about 20-30 minutes. Then take one to two hours to rate each opportunity that survived the first screening, using the format in Figure 10-1.

Finally, *down-side risk* rates the impact on the business if you had to abandon the opportunity after paying the costs associated with trying to do it. It's an estimate of what the 'sunk costs' will be. A high rating indicates that failure of the opportunity could destabilize the finances of the company. Low ratings are for those opportunities that would have little measurable impact on the financial health of the business.

After completing the ratings, review the list again with the team and sort the list into three categories. One group is the ideas that all agree do not merit further consideration. Indicate this by putting a '-' in the margin. The second group is for any idea that is clearly good, to which all team members agree to commit at the next meeting if it's of high enough priority and there are sufficient resources. Indicate this with a '+'. Note that a '+' rating is not approval of an opportunity, but just an indication that it can pass to the decision phase without further research. Ideas that are neither clearly '+' or clearly '-' get a '?' indicating that they need further research to resolve their status.

> **Outside the Meeting**
>
> At the first planning meeting, assign someone, usually the champion for the idea, the responsibility for preparing an Opportunity Screening, using the format in Figure 10-2. A screening should be done for all questionable ('?') opportunities. It may also be done in select cases for the opportunities that are deemed sound ideas ('+').

Beyond Level 2

The first two screening levels should have greatly pared down the list of viable opportunities under consideration. Once you get past a cursory look, there will be some opportunities that you should examine in greater depth. This is where you ramp up the time you spend looking at an opportunity by doing some research and a written screening, described below. (This screening is designed for market and

Date:_____
Worksheet No.: 4.4

PERCEIVED OPPORTUNITIES

Perceived Opportunities	Perceived Value	Assumed Probability of Success	Anticipated Management Effort	Perceived Down-Side Exposure
Present Business				
Improve consistency of interior coatings	2	100%	L	L
Improve burst strength limits	7	100%	L	L
Establish high-level selling program at Jones Candy	5	100%	M	L
Present Products to New Markets				
Non-food interior packaging	9	60%	M	L
Non-food exterior packaging	9	30%	H	M
Export	6	10%	M	M
Present Products for Present Market				
Tek-pak	7	50%	H	L
New Products for New Markets				
Laptop computer	10	50%	H	H
Competitive Acquisition				
Acquire ABC	2	50%	H	H
Vertical Integration				
Acquire paper mill	8	5%	H	H
Operating Improvements				
Obtain Bobst die cutter	2	100%	L	L
Refinance mortgage	1	100%	L	L

Perceived Value: 1-10, with 1 = very low
Assumed Probability of Success: 0% - 100%
Anticipated Management Effort: high, moderate, or low
Perceived Down-Side Exposure: high, moderate, or low

Figure 10-1. Perceived opportunities worksheet

OPPORTUNITY SCREENING WORKSHEET

What Is the Opportunity? Laptop computer with a 300 MHz Pentium II processor, fax/voice/data modem, IR and cellular communications capability, 13" active matrix color screen, 64MB RAM, 4.0GB removable hard drive, lithium ion battery with 10 hours of life, PCI graphics and controller with 8MB Video RAM, touchpad pointing device, CD-ROM, full multimedia.
What Is the Market Need to Be Served? Portable creativity. The complete laptop mobile office. Cellular phone/voicemail/pager. Status symbol.
What Is (Are) the Market(s) to Be Served? Business owners, high-level business executives, and sales professionals.
Is the Opportunity Compatible with Our Strategic Focus? Strategic Competencies? Mission Statement? No. It is a *very* poor fit.
How Is the Market Need Currently Being Met? There are 15 competing models (but none has all the above features).
What Product/Package Improvements Are Needed/Desired by Market? Full capabilities as listed above plus weight reduction to less than 6 lbs.
Can We Be Cost-Competitive? ???
Have We the Necessary Management Capability and Capacity? Yes
Can We Handle the Technology? We do not have the technology. This can be bought.
Can We Handle the Operations? Operations are technical purchasing and simple assembly. This is routine for us.
Can We Handle the Marketing? Do We Have Appropriate Distribution Channels? We will need to hire some top talent in this area. We should use top consultant to plan marketing strategy and develop job description and job specifications. Will need to develop a completely new sales and distribution channel.
Can We Handle the Financing? We need help even to answer the question. This could be our roadblock.
What Is the Current Size of the Market? Is It Too Large or Too Small? Current available volume: $500-700 million annual sales. It is too large unless we segment the market and create a niche. This will require solid strategy.

Figure 10-2. Opportunity screening worksheet

Is There a Competitive Opening? How Must We Position Offering to Obtain Entry? If we can make a product that meets the requirements, then it will sell in volume. Appear to be few barriers to entry. Need a market study to confirm this assessment.
Is There a Reasonable Basis for a Competitive Advantage for Us? What Strategic Competencies Are Involved? We believe that merely meeting the requirements will give us an advantage. It will require a whole new set of strategic competencies.
Is There Potential for Specialty Status for Us? Which Features or Benefits Will Command a Premium? Yes. We should get a premium for 1) high speed, 2) built-in printer, and 3) versatile communications interface.
Who Are the Most Likely Competitors? What Will Be Their Likely Competitive Response? Compaq, Dell, AST. We will be copied within one year by low-cost manufacturers.
Can We Achieve Significant/Adequate Market Penetration? Estimate Market Share for 1st and 5th years. ???
What Is the Expected Growth Rate for the Market? High–over 10%.
What Are the Expected Profit Levels for the Market? Strong at first, but weakening as competition copies us.
Are There Any Threats to the Market? Not unless there is some unforeseen disaster.
Is There Any Potential for Product or Service Displacement? Probably not displacement per se. But technical improvements are possible. We will have to be extremely responsive to avoid technical obsolescence.
What Is the Expected Return on Invested Capital? $100MM on $100MM = 100%?????
What Is the Down-Side Exposure to Financial Loss? High (Poor design, misreading the market, or sloppy execution would be disastrous. Not recovering investment in first year.)
Can We Afford the Down-Side Exposure? No. But we can avoid poor design and sloppy execution. Reading the market and the investment recovery would be serious difficulties.

Figure 10-2. (continued)

product opportunities. You may have some internal operating improvements that you should screen using a simple financial analysis.)

At the second meeting, all opportunity screenings are reviewed. These items that were questionable are now categorized as '+' or '-.' The pluses are sent on as candidates for incorporation into your vision when you get to the final strategy decisions in Chapter 14.

Make Assumptions About What Might Go Wrong

Not everything is going to be favorable to you. There are bad things that can happen to companies, and this is the time to consider those adverse things that might be in store for you.

> **Strategic Tip**
>
> People don't like to think about threats. The more bad stuff they think of, the more they want to change the subject. Expect to have to push your team to think about threats. It's important to develop an extensive list, because you will deal with those you identify—it's the ones you do not identify that will surprise you and cause the most harm. So ask your team, "What is the worst thing that can happen to us?"

The purpose of examining threats is not to scare the daylights out of you, but rather to surface the bad stuff that's lurking around in the business environment so you can do something about it before it's too late.

The important point to remember is that the threats you consider will probably be avoided, because you'll end up taking thoughtful, evasive action. Isn't that just what you expect from a sound strategy process?

When you think about threats, here are some suggestions to consider:

- What if your major customer decides to no longer buy from you?
- What if there is a natural disaster?

A Story About Assumptions

Instafoam, a small producer of high-tech packaging equipment and materials, had a close call that reinforced the importance of understanding threats. We were working with company executives at a local hotel one day and discussing that very topic. One executive said that he believed planning for every contingency was sort of overkill. He said he thought people were overly concerned about natural disasters. Honestly, 15 minutes later, the executive secretary walked into the meeting to announce that the company had closed because of a tornado that had wiped out the warehouse across the street. The cynical executive cited the near miss as an example of why the odds were so much against needing intensive insurance such as that carried by the company. Then, the director of R&D, who was ghostly pale, spoke.

> ### Strategic Tip
>
> When faced with a significant strategic threat, consider each of the following questions to minimize the impact.
> 1. Can you prevent the threat?
> 2. Can you reduce your exposure to the threat?
> 3. Can you develop some indicator to give an early warning that the threat is occurring?
> 4. What will be your contingency plan when the threat does occur?
> 5. Can you insure or hedge against the threat?

"All of our millions of dollars worth of research records were in that warehouse." And suddenly, the assumption that there could be a natural disaster didn't seem so far-fetched.

- What if there is a plane crash with all of your executives?
- What if your best factory workers hit the lottery?
- What if some technology comes along to make what you do obsolete?
- What if a government regulation turns your industry upside down?

Once you've come up with a list of threats, evaluate them to identify those that have major potential impact or that are very likely to occur. The threats that have a high impact, even if they may be unlikely to occur, are of more concern than those with a low impact. (For example, you need to check to see if your business is constructed on some sort of fault zone.) Also, you need to look at the probability of threats occurring, because if something is likely to happen, you should be ready for it.

> ### In the Meeting
>
> Ask each team member to jot down three or four things that could threaten your business. Then ask each person, in turn, to propose the most significant threat on his or her list, to build a list of about 15-20 overall threats to the business. Allocate 30-60 minutes at the second meeting to capture threats on a worksheet as shown in Worksheet 4.6 (Figure 10-3) and rate each as shown below. Highlight those threats deemed to be strategically significant and note those requiring further discussion as a *strategic issue* (see Chapter 12).

PERCEIVED THREATS

Date: _____
Worksheet No.: 4.6

Perceived Threats	Potential Impact	Assumed Probability
Fire–total loss	M	L
Loss of key employee (Joe or Ned)	H	L
Product obsolescence (paperboard dividers)	M	L
Technical obsolescence (switch to plastics)	H	L
Loss of key account (Jones)	M	M
Loss of paperboard source	M	L
Union organization attempt	M-L	L
Increased price competition	M	H
Loss of product liability insurance	L	L
Foreign competition	M	L
Brown focuses on Chicago	L	L-M
Natural disaster	M	L
Recession	L	L

Potential Impact: high, moderate, or low
Assumed Probability: high, moderate, or low

Figure 10-3. Perceived threats worksheet

So it's time to brainstorm. Make a list of threats that you're worried about and rate them.

Now, you have a clear idea of the opportunities and threats that lie in your future. You're thinking about what might happen and how you can take advantage of it. You're doing it in a three- to five-year range, and yet the future will actually last longer than that. We have found that the spectacular winners are those who can see far into the future and set themselves up before others are even awake to the coming changes. The future that seems so distant now will at some point become the present. And just imagine if you started preparing now.

chapter 11

Look Further into the Future

TOMORROW DOESN'T JUST HAPPEN TOMORROW. It happens the next day too. If you can figure out what's going to happen long-term before anyone else figures it out, you have a chance to own Boardwalk in the Monopoly game of business. Of course, no one really knows what's going to happen, so you need to make a bit of a guess. This means that in most cases you should avoid devoting excessive resources to divining the future, but it also means you do need to think about it.

Make an educated guess, think about it, and move on. In most cases, your first, instinctive assumption will be as good as one you agonized over for hours. Just make the assumptions and remember to review them now and then.

Most assumptions are made with a three- to five-year time horizon. This is with good reason. Three to five years is generally considered the relevant strategic time horizon. But if you look only at that short chunk of time, you may miss some larger trends coming down the pike. If you don't look at the big trends, in three to five years you'll be starting to look at trouble instead, because even though a trend may not lead to much for a little while, when it does you may need time to catch up.

Don't fall asleep. You can't afford to fall asleep today and awaken in complete ignorance of tomorrow. The big changes may completely rule your life in the future, so don't bury your head in the sand. Look at today. Look at tomorrow. Whatever you do, don't become complacent and ignore the changes the future is bringing. If you do, it's a nap you'll regret all the way to the bank.

We recommend spending one good hour thinking about the big trends that affect your industry. That's all you need for now.

The Big Picture—What's Going to Happen in the World?

Seeing things ahead of time gives you an advantage.

If an asteroid were heading toward the Earth and you had a big enough telescope to pick it up five years before it would arrive, there's a chance you could do something to avoid it or at least mitigate the negative impact. Better yet, you might even find a way to harness the energy of the thing as it passed close by and turn it into an opportunity. But if you didn't pick it up until the last minute, there's probably not much you could do but hope it would miss.

Here's another example, more down to earth. It's 1993 and you produce tires. Somebody comes to you and declares that sports utility vehicles will be all the rage in five years. If you heed that advice, you can figure out that you'll need new machines or at least a change of production in order to serve this new market.

Once again, the big picture down the road covers the same elements as the big picture in shorter time horizons:

- Markets
- Competition
- Technology
- Supplier Markets
- Government Regulations
- Economy

When you think about the big picture, what you want is a sense of where the world is going. For such a long time horizon, you don't necessarily need to look at things as opportunities or threats. After all, you can make a threat into an opportunity or, if you behave inappropriately, you can make an opportunity into a threat. Instead, you just want to understand future implications of current trends and then think about appropriate responses. If you see a change coming and you start adapting today, you can succeed.

Imagine Now from 10 Years Ago

Your goal is to write a scenario of where the industry will be in 10 years. In order to do that, a constructive exercise is to remember how much change actually happens in that amount of time.

So think back a decade.

First, technology was in the Stone Age compared with the present. In 1989, 9600-baud modems were available and cost about $800. At the time, a 25 megahertz Intel 80386 microprocessor was considered blazingly fast. 386 laptops—when you could find them—weighed over 15 pounds, had monochrome screens, and cost over $3,000. A hand-held cellular phone wouldn't fit into your pocket but would set you back $1,500. In fact, everything technological was bigger, slower, and more expensive. And, of course, the only people who were really aware of the Internet were serious geeks. America Online felt it was doing well when it topped 250,000 subscribers.

> **Tales from the Strategy Vault**
>
> Think about college freshmen, the ones you'll be employing in a few years. They were born in the early 1980s. They have never known a world without AIDS and the Soviet Union came apart when they were just children. To them, the Vietnam War is ancient history. They have never lived in a world without environmental regulations. Most have probably never lived in a house without a VCR or an answering machine. Think of that perspective and compare it with yours. The world changes.

At the time, the country was still fighting the Cold War and deficits were high. Beanie Babies and the Furby had not yet been invented. The Home Shopping Club was poised to take over the economy. From the consequential to the trivial, the world was significantly different 10 years ago.

But that's the past, the easy part. What about the future?

This exercise is a way to begin thinking about the future and what might be in store. It's most likely going to look more different than you think. By understanding the magnitude of change over the past 10 years, you can get a calibration on what to expect in the next 10 years. Don't just think of global terms; think of things that are specific to your particular industry. What's going to be different?

What's going to happen to the people who are your current customers?

- Are they going to buy from the same channels?
- Will they need the same kind of product?
- What will they be thinking about in terms of needs in your industry?
- What will they demand of a company like yours?

> **Tales from the Strategy Vault**
>
> In the late 1970s, overnight delivery services were developed to fill the need of the time-sensitive legal and financial industries. Some forward-looking retail catalog merchants realized they could gain significant advantage by using these new services. Within 20 years "overnight" became the norm in almost all industries. Do you think there is a parallel with the rise of the Internet—developed in the 1980s to allow rapid and easy exchange of data in the academic communities? What developments that lie outside your industry today will become key drivers in the coming decades?

Look into your industry. What is going on? What is going to go on?

Look at current trends and extrapolate them out 10 years and try to figure what things will look like. Will things level off or will they accelerate?

Look outside your industry. Some things that start outside of your industry will become significant factors within your industry. What's gone on in the last 10 years? Where is it all leading? Progress stops for no one.

There is *stuff* going on that you should at least contemplate. For instance, consider:

- What happens if the notion of outsourced warehousing, as is done by L.L. Bean and Lands' End, comes to your industry?
- What happens if quality levels such as those pursued by Motorola get pushed into your industry?
- What happens if General Electric's pursuit of recasting businesses as financing and service providers takes hold in your industry?
- Could your business be replaced by a Web site?
- Is there anything that can't be leased?

Winner's Profile in the New World

Once you've thought about what the world is going to look like in 10 years, you then want to figure out who is going to win—and how.

If you can create a profile of a winner in this new environment, you can begin to put yourself on the road to fitting that profile. What are the characteristics of a winning company in your scenario of the future? Who is going to win? How?

INDUSTRY SCENARIO

Date: _____
Worksheet No.: 4.7

- Domestic confectionery industry grows 3% per year.
- Bakery industry grows by 5% per year.
- More plastic.
- Few large suppliers of commodity packaging.
- Limited, no-growth market for specialty suppliers.
- Greater automation and higher speeds.
- New technical requirements.
- Recyclable/degradable packaging.

Figure 11-1. Industry scenario worksheet

If you can get your team to think about and sketch out a winning company in that environment, you can get your team thinking about becoming that winning company.

For each of the items in your industry scenario, ask this question: If what we predict were to come to pass, what would be the essential characteristics of a winning company?

Once you've created a list of attributes that will help you become a winner in that scenario of the future, rate how important those attributes are. Then, rate your current per-

formance. You're trying to get a fix on the gap between your current performance and your desired performance. This is just one way to highlight areas where your company may want to grow new capabilities. This will help you formulate strategy as you go forward.

The whole point of this is not to form a precise picture of the distant future. After all, you may be wrong. But you want to spend a half-hour on this in your meeting to make people aware that this stuff must be considered. All you really want to do is create a fuzzy picture of the future. And then you want to ask the question: Are there things that we can start to learn or do today that can put us in a position to be a big winner in the future?

Some companies have substantial risks that they must consider. For instance, Thorpe Corporation has a division that does construction inside petrochemical heaters. It's a demanding job in a potentially dangerous environment and it requires skills. The company often has trouble finding people who have the skills and are willing want to work in these conditions, no matter how much it pays. Thorpe can look into the future and know that any winning profile will include the ability to attract qualified workers. So this company has begun working on a way to create and maintain a sufficient labor pool, an ongoing strategy of attracting young people. It's only beginning to pay off, but it will work with some fine-tuning. And it's better than doing nothing. Winners act on their visions.

This rating is a very tough test. You will be rating your performance today against where you think the winner will be in the future. Such a tough test is sure to spark some creative thoughts about what you have to

---

Tales from the Strategy Vault

A customer in the printing business who attended one of our first seminars seemed to have learned a bit about anticipating the future. At the time, he was running a printing plant and he decided to invest money in computers before most printing plants would even consider it. "It was scary," he told us later. "But I just felt it was right. It was where the print industry was going." He envisioned this was what a successful printer would be doing 10 years in the future— and invested money to match his vision. He was on target and he mopped up, shutting his competitors out of most of the key big contracts in his markets. He continues to do so because he now has a lock on the high end of the market in his area.

In the Meeting

During the second meeting, ask your team to develop a *winner's profile*, as shown in Figure 11-2. You should spend about 20 minutes developing the characteristics of a winner from the scenario developed for the worksheet in Figure 11-1. Then take 15-25 minutes to rate your performance and the importance and to identify critical gaps. Be sure to develop the winner's profile from the industry scenario (Figure 11-1), not some assumed wish list.

WINNER'S PROFILE

Date: _____
Worksheet No.: 4.8

Characteristic	Future Importance	Current Performance
Flexible Manufacturing	2	6
Knowledge of Plastics Technology	1	5
Product Quality	2	3
Joint Venture for Materials Development	3	3
Environmentally Friendly Products	3	2
Participative/TQM Culture	2	7
Cost-Effective Manufacturing	2	4
Integrated Use of Current Information Systems Technology	2	6
Interior Packaging Design Expertise	2	2
Exterior Packaging Design Expertise	2	3

Importance
1 Extremely Critical
2 Very Critical
3 Critical
4 Extremely Important
5 Very Important
6 Important
7 Extremely Beneficial
8 Very Beneficial
9 Beneficial

Performance
1 Almost Perfect
2 Excellent
3 Good
4 Some Strength (on the balance)
5 Neutral
6 Some Weakness (on the balance)
7 Poor
8 Very Poor
9 Abysmal

Figure 11-2. Winner's profile worksheet

do to close the gaps—and that's just what you want. It's time now to get beyond the analysis and begin to craft your course and direction—to set strategy for the enterprise.

Part Four

Design Your Future

NOW IT'S TIME TO DESIGN YOUR FUTURE. It's time to crystallize that vision and develop your cultural commitments throughout the company. It's time to turn your vision into reality.

But first there will be a few issues to resolve. You know those big questions that have been boiling up with each part of the planning process? So far, we've been holding them off, waiting until we had agreement on our facts and assumptions. Now it's time. In this section you will dig into the gritty details and make the tough choices that establish your vision. If you're not making choices, you're not doing strategy. That's a simple and profound fact.

There will be choices of focus and assessment of markets. You will have to select some markets and opportunities for expansion or vigorous defense, while realizing that others will have to go with fewer resources to support such aggressive campaigns. You will have issues of what competencies to build and what capabilities are required. Issues of people and financial resources may also surface. We will lead you through a systematic resolution of all of these issues that will establish your vision. Then it's time to write it all down—to finalize your strategy.

But a three- to five-year strategy is nothing but hollow words if there's not a true commitment throughout the organization to support that strategy. To establish that commitment, you will need to develop a mission statement, some goals, and a few definitive objectives to achieve in the short run. These will lead you to more than words on paper—they will ensure results.

chapter 12

Declare a
Strategic Focus

T OO MANY COMPANIES DON'T FOCUS. They don't remember that you can get very good at one thing if you just focus on it. Or they have that famous Ph.D. fear—that they will know *so much* about *so little* that they will have one customer love them to death. It's a legitimate concern, but no reason to avoid focus. It hardly ever happens.

Think about 20 people in one room. What if the door were locked and they wanted to get out? They could all run in different directions and slam their shoulders into the wall. Or they could concentrate on one particular area. Even better, if they had a tool, they could slam away at that one area until they smashed a hole through the wall. In many endeavors, a tight focus with all energy channeled in one direction is the key to breaking out of the box.

In business, you win when you bring more talent to bear on an issue critical to your customer than anyone else in the market. Let's say that again so it sinks in … *more* talent, *more* resources, *more* of something that matters (a lot) to the customer, than anyone else.

Some think that all it takes is "a few" resources or "enough to match the other guy"—but those strategies are dangerous. Too little clout in a market usually leads to being trapped in an undesirable third- or fourth-tier position (unless you are woefully underpositioned, in which case a swift death can be merciful). Just matching a competitor leaves customers to select a vendor on price alone, driving profits out of the market and locking both parties into a slow, frustrating death dance.

There are two ways to increase your clout in a market: you can *buy* your way in by pouring tons of resources into gaining a better position or you can *focus* your way in by shrinking your definition of the target market so as to ensure that your current resources will give you the strongest position. Either strategy can be successful since each achieves dominance in the target market. One takes a big bag of money, which is fine if you have one. The other takes some time and intelligence to figure out the market. Which will it be for you? We think focus is to be cherished—even for very large businesses.

What do you sell? Who are your target customers?

Those two questions may seem obvious and a lot of companies can probably give those questions a quick answer. But few companies are focused enough to smash away at one thing that could make them a sure winner. Too many companies try to be all things to all people and spread themselves too thin. This lack of focus lets a company dabble in many available markets, but it doesn't drive a company to a commanding position within its chosen markets. Focus is critical to giving your company a chance for big success.

So, here's a critical piece of advice: *Find something that is critical to your customers, and define a focus around it such that you can bring more talent, more resources to bear on it that anyone else.*

All successful companies find some way to establish dominance in their markets:

> ## Tales from the Strategy Vault
>
> Back in Chapter 6 we told of the battle of Thermopylae, in which a small Spartan army was able to hold off the vastly larger Persian army by choosing a narrow pass as the battle site. The Spartans used the concept of focus, their intelligence, and their knowledge of their home geography to select a battlefield that favored their troops. They selected a pass that was small enough for them to dominate and kept the Persian army from using all its soldiers. This choice created a battle that favored the Spartan strength in one-to-one combat. An alternative might have been available to the Spartans. They could have spent all of their treasury hiring enough mercenaries to match the larger invading army. Matching the Persians would have given them equal odds of holding off the invaders: they might have won, but they might have lost. And in either case they would have had a problem of getting the hordes of mercenaries out of their country when the battle was done. Which strategy would you have chosen?

- Small companies should try to dominate small markets.
- Large companies should try to dominate big markets.

Who Are You?

Although the question of focus is "Who are you?" the real question might be better phrased "Who aren't you?"

Focus is about drawing lines and understanding what you do by knowing very clearly what you do not do. Your efforts can be diluted over a wide range of customers. And if you lose focus you can lose profitability.

One of our clients had a VP of sales who used to be a car salesman, who demonstrated a clear understanding of the need to focus. Now, most people would think that a car salesman would try to sell a car to every person who came into the showroom with a pulse. But this par-

> ### Strategic Tip
>
> Pick a cliché; they all apply—"spreading yourself too thin," "biting off more than you can chew," "being all things to all people." All these expressions speak to a common problem: lack of focus. Or, think of it this way: you can shoot at a whole bunch of targets or you can shoot at a few targets a whole bunch of times. Usually, if you study a target for a while, you get better at hitting it. That's focus.

ticular car salesman was very particular about whom he approached. See, he sold Porsches in a dealership that shared space with Volkswagen. And every time a customer came through the door, this car salesman had to decide whether that person was his customer or not. Either a potential customer had $80,000 for a Porsche 911 or the person had only $8,000 and merely wanted to test drive the 911 before buying a Volkswagen Jetta. And so he studied human nature and made intelligent guesses on which people to approach and whom to let be. That's how he did it. He knew he sold Porsches.

So what is your focus? What do you sell? Who are your customers? As things are narrowed, the picture of what you do becomes clearer. You get better at it because you know it. And if you are not confused by chasing some new rainbow every day, you will get even better at whatever it is that you do well. So if you sell Porsches, concentrate on Porsche customers. You will be much better off than if you were to concentrate on *people who want to buy a car*. That would not be much focus.

A Story About Furniture

We have a 100-year-old family-owned furniture company as a client. It took this company, Bernhardt Furniture, a few years of working with this process, but it eventually became a model for how to take success, focus it, and then watch it explode.

When we first started working with these people, they defined their company as being in the furniture business. They had product offerings for every room in a home at high and more moderate price points. They had case goods and upholstery in all kinds of styles—18th century, American traditional, contemporary, and more. They were up against the big names in the industry. They were competing, in their own words, against big names like Thomasville, Lexington, Stanley, Henredon, Century ... and the list went on. But most of these competitors were five, 10, or 20 times bigger than they were and they commanded considerably more attention in the retail channels.

The Bernhardt team had noble dreams. But while they'd had periods of strong success in their 100-year history, the reality was that they had, in fact, cornered way under 1% of the broad furniture market. They were the little fish in the big pond and the business was slowly eroding on many fronts, taking a toll on corporate profitability. They were in the game, but not really competing in any effective way with the big guys. Working with the simplified strategic planning process, they began to narrow their market down. They were able to say that they made high-end furniture, but that focus was still too broad to have much effect on their performance.

As they analyzed their situation, it became clear to them that a lot of the furniture game is about "floor space." They needed retail visibility—floor space at the dealers—and it was tough to get that space because it was mostly taken up by the big guys. And they had a tough time getting the dealers to notice them because their product was a "me-too" offering. It was as good as the others, but not distinctive. If a dealer had a choice between Bernhardt Furniture or one of the better known brands, such as Thomasville or Lexington, the dealer invariably selected the better-known brand. So Bernhardt was getting second-tier and third-tier distribution in every city. They made a comfortable living, but it wasn't the business they wanted it to be.

And then...

They completely transformed their company. We will not kid you. It was in many ways gut-wrenching. But the more they studied the market, the less nostalgia mattered and the more the light bulb over their heads inspired them. They saw it!

They saw that focus held the key to success. With a critical eye they identified what was working, what strategic competencies they had, and where these could bring them success in the market. They worked on these and little else. They became great at a particular kind of furniture. So good, in fact, that if you wanted to be a comprehensive furniture dealer, you *had* to have Bernhardt in your showroom. The most important factor in their focusing was scaling down and seeking to dominate. They went from being irrelevant to being crucial. They are now *the company* for this type of furniture and, as you might expect, all of the usual indicators of success are on a positive trend. Focus changed the company. While most companies in the furniture industry are struggling in the competition, Bernhardt flourishes.

Can There Be Too Much Focus?

On occasion, a company is right to fear the Ph.D. phenomenon—knowing too much about too little. It's rare, but worth mentioning.

A good example is a company that makes only toy soldiers. In the modern age of computers and high-tech talking animals, there's not much of a market for toy soldiers. There may be a few hundred thousand people who collect toy soldiers: it's a pretty esoteric hobby. But it's a market and at least one company, Britains, attracts a lot of collectors and makes decent money. However, a few hundred thousand people don't make for a big enough market for a bunch of niches. If, somehow, a new player were able to sell a very low volume of product at very high margins, there might be enough money in the market to support another business. But otherwise, the focus may be too small to sustain a viable, growing business.

Again, we stress that this situation of too narrow a focus is rare. For almost all companies, the problem is that the focus is too broad. As your focus gets tighter, your batting average goes up. As your focus gets closer, so does your knowledge and abilities. You just don't want to focus too close on any one customer.

Too much can be a legitimate fear. But usually it's a ridiculous fear perpetuated by salespeople who would rather sell everything than sell specific things. The truth is that more focus almost always leads to more profits.

Your Choices Are Here

Every company needs to have a clear idea of what it will sell and to whom. These two points define what it will do, and what it will not do. In short, they define its *strategic focus*. (The concept we call "strategic focus" was originally developed by Ben Tregoe and John Zimmerman in their book, *Top Management Strategy* (Simon and Schuster, 1980), as "driving force.")

There are six kinds of strategic focus that make sense for mid-sized or smaller companies and divisions of large companies:

- products/services
- capabilities
- markets/customers
- technology
- raw material supply
- method of sale/distribution

Now, many of these areas have great importance to most companies. Take your company, for example. You probably have a product or service to sell and you must sell to customers who make up a market. You likely have some capabilities or technologies that you use to create your offering. In many cases you will use some distribution channel or method of sale. You may use even primary raw materials. So if companies have all of these, where is the focus? How does this work?

The point of strategic focus is that you must select one of these things to be "primary." The question that you must ask yourself about strategic focus is what is the one part of your business that you will stay true to no matter what? The one you select sets the bounds for what you will do and for whom you will do it. You choose to have a tight focus on the selected category, while allowing for much greater range of variability in the other categories. Let's look at some examples.

Products and Services

If your company focuses on products and services, you define what you will do by your product or service category. You think first about making that product or service better. You might sell your offering to a rather wide range of markets or customers, perhaps through a variety of distribution channels. You might use various capabilities or technologies to create your offering, but you would offer only a fairly narrow range of products or services that fit your defined strategic focus.

Think, for instance, of Boeing. A huge company, right? And yet, it's driven by its products and services. That defines what it does and what it doesn't do. You can pretty much bet that the next product that Boeing Corporation puts out will be some kind of airframe or aerospace product. It will probably have wings and it will probably fly through the air. That's what they do. They know it, you know it, and they know that you know it. In fact, they like that you know that.

Boeing, no doubt, could make trains if they wanted. But they don't. They make planes, and they seem quite content in their growing little business.

Capabilities

A company that selects capabilities as its strategic focus defines what it will do by its set of capabilities. A general machine shop is a good example of this sort of focus. It will take on jobs that match the equipment and tooling it has and it will refuse those that don't fit its capabilities. It doesn't matter what the product is or what the customer does.

The down side of a capabilities strategic focus is that it's difficult to avoid falling into commodity status, selling machine hours or labor hours. If you choose capabilities as your focus, you have to be sure to be specific enough to avoid facing the entire world as your competition.

Most companies that choose capabilities wrongly choose "whatever" as their capability. In other

> **Tales from the Strategy Vault**
>
> We once worked with a company involved in the chemical industry that could put all sorts of things through their plant—perfumes, glue, paint, or whatever. And that was their attitude—"whatever." But they had an advantage they had never realized before. When asked, they said that they were consistently hitting high quality levels, stuff like 99.999%—always. This was huge capability for many customers. When this company focused on customers that needed such quality, it could charge more and attract more specific customers.

words, when asked what they can do well, they answer, "We do whatever you want in this area." For instance, think of an accounting firm that specializes in "whatever you want." Gosh, how many of those are there?

But if you were to choose accounting for health care firms, for example, suddenly you may have a specialty that makes you much more valuable. Sure, you become less valuable to most of the population, but they weren't going to buy your services anyway. What matters is that you're more valuable to health care firms. How about accounting for movie theaters? That could work. You have credibility in a specific area that commands some kind of premium. And you're a specialist company. Is that valuable? You bet it is.

Markets and Customers

A strategic focus on markets and customers begins with a well-defined group of potential buyers. You strive to understand and satisfy their particular needs. With a markets and customers focus, you're willing to consider a broader array of products, capabilities, and other things in order to deliver the highest value to the chosen market or customers. When you focus on a well-defined group of customers, it's possible to provide those customers with an offer that they value much more than those of narrow product- or capabilities-focused competitors.

> **Tales from the Strategy Vault**
>
> If you own a contracting company, you absolutely must have a W.W. Grainger catalog: the company sells almost everything a contractor needs. If you want a piece of equipment, you can find it in the 2,000-page catalog. This is a company that is absolutely focused on its market and customers. This focus has made its catalog into a Bible of the trade.

Distribution companies often have a markets/customers focus. One of our colleagues worked for a company that sells a wide range of products to dentists and dental labs. Founded over 100 years ago, this company started out selling a dental molding compound (a product focus). As their salespeople called on dentists, they discovered that the small practices needed tools to clean the molding compound from the teeth after use and they needed trays to hold the molding compound. As time went by, the company took advantage of opportunities to sell the dentists items unrelated to the original compound: anesthetic, filling materials, x-ray film, cleaning solutions, etc.—anything that a dentist might use. It was a natural evolution from a product focus (how to manufacture, market, and sell the molding compound) to a markets/customers focus (we know dentists: how can we meet a broader array of their needs?).

Distributors are not the only companies that have a markets and customers strategic focus. Companies that focus on things for demographic groups (kids, older people, students, etc.) often have this focus. So do contract manufacturers or service providers that choose to address one industry or customer group with a relatively wide array of offerings that are optimized for those customers. For example, an employee benefits firm that is focused on the smaller companies might offer health insurance, outsourced payroll services, consulting, executive compensation plans, salary research, benchmarking, and more—all optimized and bundled for its smaller client companies.

Technology

There are a lot of high-tech companies, but not many companies that have a technology strategic focus. Such a focus limits you to a particular technology.

Many mistakenly think a company such as Intel is a technology-focused company. The truth is that, although Intel utilizes a lot of technology, the company has a strategic focus on products and services. Intel makes microprocessors. It's products and not technology that limits what Intel will do and for whom. If the most effective technology for making computer chips moved from silicon-based to carbon-based processing, you can bet Intel would adapt to carbon-based technology. Intel invests billions each year to keep up with changing technology, all so it can make one product category, microprocessors, better than anyone else.

Millipore, a scientific company headquartered near Boston, is one of the best examples of a technology strategic focus. Millipore has some of the world's best knowledge of high-performance filtration for purifying water and other liquids. All of its activities revolve around filtration. As a testament to this focus, the company has divested of a division that was a leader in chromatography, a related but different technology.

> ### Tales from the Strategy Vault
>
> In the early years of the Manhattan Project, a private company developed centrifuge technology to refine uranium to build the atomic bomb. But after World War II, the government and the Atomic Energy Commission made that job of refining uranium a government-controlled project, so this company needed a new direction. It focused on the technology of the centrifuge and found there were many fields with a need for centrifuge separation. Blood analysis and DNA separation were just two areas this company has branched into while maintaining a focus on its core technology.

Biotechnology companies are very often technology-focused. They develop a specific technology at which they can excel and apply this technology to a wide range of produces and markets. Whether it's working on cures for human disease, transgenetic soybeans, or bacteria that synthesize plastics, they seek applications of their core technology to make a big profit.

Raw Materials

If your focus is raw materials, it means that you will do most anything to do with your raw material and its downstream products. For instance, Georgia-Pacific is a company that makes stuff from trees. If it comes from a tree, talk to Georgia-Pacific. The company will make lumber, forest product chemicals, paper, and pulp. It does it all.

Energy companies like Exxon-Mobil and Shell are the same. They don't care what they make as long as it somehow starts with a barrel of oil.

A company that attended our seminar last year specializes in recycling a particular material and making a variety of products for a variety of markets using the output material from its recycling process. The company will make anything, as long as the products come from its recycled materials. Its strategic focus is raw materials.

Sales and Distribution

If your sales or distribution channel defines what you will do or not do, then you have a sales and distribution strategic focus. You don't care what it is that you move as long as it can move through your channel and you get your cut. Maybe you have a particular method of reaching customers. The Home Shopping Network is an example. So is Amway. Many of the Internet companies are following a sales and distribution strategic focus.

Choose Here

So those are the six options. The strategic challenge for you is to choose one of these things, not many of them. If you choose several of these, you don't really have a focus.

Although it can be tempting to declare no focus and instead say you will be opportunistic, that doesn't work as well as a clear focus. Companies with no focus are difficult places to work. There are conflicting agendas and confused signals. Employees are caught switching hats as they try to serve the rigors of multiple focuses. One minute they're working on new products for a market, only to be pulled off the next moment to work on new markets for existing products. Everyone gets stretched too thin as they attempt to be all things to all people. And one of the most telling signs of a lack of focus is poor profitability.

As two brothers we worked with discovered, you have to have a tight focus if you want to have a successful business.

Two Brothers and One Company

Once upon a time, there was a company that made fluid processing equipment for the dairy market. These were machines that could automate the process of getting milk from a cow to tanks ready to go to market. One day, the man who started the company died and it was passed along to his two sons.

One son had spent a lot of time when he was growing up working with the salespeople. He had called on many dairy farmers in his time and he really knew what they wanted. He knew, *just knew*, that farmers would be open to an expansion of products. He thought that the best way to improve the business and move it forward with the next generation of leadership was to broaden the product line and do all sorts of stuff focused on the dairy farm market. He saw a business of mops, pails, uniforms, tanks, coolers—lots of dairy stuff.

The other son had spent a lot of time when he was growing up working with the technology side of the business. He really knew the technology of milking machines, and he *just knew* that the basic instrumentation for handling milk could be easily adapted to beverages, fluid food products, chemicals, pharmaceuticals, or any other fluid. He envisioned a product line that would handle all sorts of fluid processing.

In spite of an 80% share in its base market, the company was having trouble with profitability because the two brothers were driving it in quite different directions. Each vision required significant resources and neither received full endorsement because it was competing with the other. Both were viewed as absolutely valid. Both floundered.

The brothers had to pick and finally they picked the products focus—selling high-quality fluid food processing equipment. The minute they made the decision, everything fell into place. All energies went in one direction.

In the Meeting

During the second meeting, you will want to discuss and resolve your future strategic focus. Include "What should be our future strategic focus?" as one of the top strategic issues on the worksheet in Figure 12-1.

During the strategic issues discussion, review the merits and applicability of each of the six types of strategic focus detailed above and discuss these with your team. Select the focus to which you will hold true above all of the others. The selected focus should be able to complete this phrase, "We don't care what it is; as long as it is _____, we will consider doing it."

Be sure that this topic gets sufficient discussion so that all team members fully understand and buy into the strategic implications of the selected focus.

Strategic Issues

Resolving strategic focus is a critical issue for any company. In fact, we are at the point in the process where there are many critical issues that you have to sort out in order to establish a strategy. If you've been working this process to its full potential, your team should be primed with a number of issues that have been raised by the research and discussions up to this point:

- What should be our strategic focus?
- Which markets are most attractive for us to pursue?
- How are we going to achieve dominance over competitors in our market segments?
- Which opportunities will give us the greatest return?
- How can we take advantage of our strengths and minimize our weaknesses?

These questions are examples of *strategic issues*, those critical questions that you need to answer so that you can all agree on a strategy. With these and other issues on everyone's mind, it's time to shift gears from analysis into decision making. It's time to "tee up" the tough questions and begin to resolve them.

As we go through the next several chapters working toward the final strategy, you should begin to capture a list of strategic issues. In the "In the Meeting" boxes that accompany the text we will remind you to capture the most common issues.

Introduce this concept early in the process. Ask team members to title a note page "strategic issues." You can use this page as a "parking lot" for collecting those critical course and direction questions we need to return to later in the process. The resolution to these issues will give you a "first pass" strategy that we will then refine further and formalize in Chapter 14.

STRATEGIC ISSUES

Date: _____
Worksheet No.: 5.2

1. What should be our future *strategic focus*?
   - Our current focus is one of Products/Services
   - We have opportunities to broaden the use of our capacity and become capabilities-focused. Could lead to a strictly "commodity" orientation.
   - The most leveraged use of our strategic competencies will be to keep our Products/Services focus in the future

2. What *strategic competencies* will we require in the future?
   - Interior packaging design expertise
   - Exterior packaging appearance
   - Cost-effective manufacturing
   - Plastic packaging expertise

3. How will we build the required expertise in plastics technology to address threat?
   - Hire a commercial development manager for plastics packaging
   - Identify the specific areas of plastics packaging that would fit with our manufacturing competencies and customer profiles
   - Identify joint venture or acquisition candidates that could speed up our learning curve in the identified areas

4. Do we have sufficient growth in our core business, or is there a gap with our expectations?
   - Growth rates taper off after 2-3 years (see Growth Estimate on page 8.4-1)
   - Need to commit to opportunities to sustain the pace of growth

5. What is our role in non-food interior packaging?
   - This is a much more cost-sensitive business; does not utilize our competencies
   - A few areas (medical) do need our hygienic capabilities
   - Should identify and investigate areas that value and match our competencies
   - Do not enter general non-food commodity business

6. Do we launch the Tek-pak product line?
   - Market studies predict we could achieve $3.5M sales within 4 years
   - Market is expected to grow at 20% for next 3-5 years.
   - Expect to generate $200K in cash flow and 15% net profit before tax
   - Raising required capital of $1.2M is the only thing holding us back
   - Expected to generate 50 new jobs; should be able to get $500K state financing
   - Could refinance mortgage on plant #1 and raise balance
   - Agreed: we should pursue these means of financing and commit to project this year

7. Do we have the ability to penetrate Canadian market?
   - Do not have sufficient information to resolve this now

Figure 12-1. Strategic issues worksheet (continued on page 148)

- What is the size of the market within 300 miles of our Detroit plant?
- What are the import/export requirements?
- What will be the effect of NAFTA?

8. What are the keys to achieving a more flexible manufacturing operation?
   - Establish EDI with key customers and suppliers
   - Investigate new MRP software
   - Implement a key supplier partnership program
   - Cross train manufacturing personnel

9. How do we ensure that we have timely and accurate information for business management?

Figure 12-1. (continued)

Here's the Pot of Gold—Align Focus with Competencies

As we've reminded you on numerous occasions, there are three key strategic questions that every business must figure out:

- What are you going to sell?
- Who are your target customers?
- How will you beat or avoid the competition?

Figuring out your strategic focus resolves the first two questions. The last question involves selecting your strategic competencies. Every business should seek consistency and compatibility between its strategic focus and its strategic competencies (Figure 12-2). Get these aligned and you've set yourself up for some great times. That alignment is powerful. If you have a unique way of creating value for the customers that's difficult to copy—a competency—and it aligns with your focus, your chances of profitability skyrocket. We can't overstate that point. Your chances of making lots and lots of money skyrocket!

In the Meeting

Set up the Strategic Issues page as shown in the worksheet in Figure 12-1. Ask each team member to identify what they feel are the top two or three issues. Be sure to consider all of the topics raised in Chapters 12-14. Initially, just list the questions and organize them in priority order. Then spend up to a full day of the middle meeting discussing and resolving as many as possible in the time allocated.

Be sure that this topic gets sufficient discussion so that all team members fully understand and buy into the strategic implications of the selected strategic competencies. With the "big picture" view of your course and direction resolved in the selected strategic focus and strategic competencies, it's now the time to work out the detailed vision for each market segment in your core business.

> ## In the Meeting
>
> During the second meeting, list identification of your future strategic competencies (on the worksheet in Figure 12-1) as one of the top strategic issues for your team to resolve. Review the current strategic competencies from the worksheet in Figure 7-2. Consider this list and other strategic competencies that might be required (see Winner's Profile worksheet, Figure 11-2). Determine what will be the one to three strategic competencies that are compatible with your selected strategic focus and to which you will commit to building to world-class status over the coming years.

Strategic Focus	Typical Areas for Strategic Competencies	Typical Basis of Competitive Advantage
Products/ Services	Product Design and Development Quality Service Product Marketing	▪ Best-in-class services/products ▪ Identifying new geographic markets or classes of customers ▪ Continuous product improvement
Capabilities	Cost Leadership Efficient Process Design Substitute Marketing	▪ Low-cost process technology ▪ High-capacity utilization ▪ Flexibility in use of resources
Markets/ Customers	End-user Market Research Creating Brand Loyalty Customer Service Internal Market Analysis–MIS	▪ Best total knowledge of user group ▪ Customer-driven organization ▪ Customer intimacy ▪ Short product commercialization
Technology	Basic or Applied Research Applications Marketing Access to Capital Joint Venture and Alliance Formation	▪ Creation of markets ▪ State-of-the-art offerings ▪ World-class research capability
Raw Material Supply	Exploration/Cultivation Process Capabilities	▪ Quality, quantity, and location of resources ▪ Control of resources
Method of Sale or Distribution	Sales Recruitment and Training Systems to Track Distribution Purchasing	▪ Efficient/cost-effective sales ▪ Ability to handle wide array of products

Figure 12-2. Strategic focus, strategic competency, and competitive advantage

chapter 13

Take It All Into Account

I T'S TIME FOR STRATEGY—TIME TO FIGURE OUT WHERE YOU'RE GOING! Until now, we've been gathering information and making assumptions about the future. Now it's time to pull it all together and make some clear decisions. This is how simple strategy can be if you just go at it one step at a time.

In this chapter, you will find two types of tools: tools to help you digest the information you've gathered up to this point in the process and tools to help you set a course and direction for your organization based upon an understanding of that information.

Strategic Assessment—Charting It Out

What direction do you want to go in those market segments you have chosen? Well, before you can figure that out, it helps to understand two things: the attractiveness of the market segments and your competitive position.

When assessing any market segment, these two factors can have a strong impact on where you focus your efforts. Either of these can be strong or weak (Figure 13-1).

Naturally, we would like to have a strong competitive position in all segments, but we don't usually start out there. To build competitive position

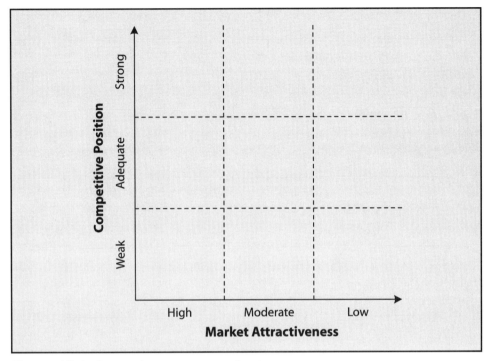

Figure 13-1. Strategic assessment chart

requires the investment of time, money, and attention. Likewise, we would like all of our markets to be very attractive, but this also is not always the case. Our strategic choices will affect both of these positions over time, but we should also consider these positions when making strategic choices. So let's look at the factors we use to judge each of these.

Market Attractiveness

Are your market segments attractive? Would an unbiased outsider consider any of your market segments a good investment? Remember: you do not have a lot of control over market attractiveness, but you have some control on how you face the competition. So, the key is to invest more time and money in markets that are attractive.

Market attractiveness has nothing to do with how well you compete in the market. It doesn't even have anything to do with your presence in the market. It's simply a subjective measure of a particular market based on four key factors of market attractiveness:

- Rate of Future Real Industry Market Volume Growth for Our Products in This Market Segment
- Average Future Industry Profit Level for Our Products in This Market Segment
- Major Threats to Market
- Potential for Product Displacement

If you followed our directions, you've identified six or eight market segments (Chapter 4) and developed some assumptions about each (Chapter 9). Now we analyze those markets without regard to any bias from your own company. The question is simply "Is it a good market?"

Would it be a good investment to do business in that segment? Of course, this depends on the required investment and the return. But the important thing to remember when considering the attractiveness of a market is not whether it's attractive to your company, but whether it's attractive as a market in general, to an outsider.

Competitive Position

How do you stack up against the competition? How would an unbiased customer rate your company relative to your competitors?

Competitive position is a relative rating. Unlike market attractiveness, which has everything to do with the market and nothing to do with your participation in it, competitive position has everything to do with how you stack up against others who want the same customers as you. You want to rate yourself (as objectively as possible) against the competition on seven key characteristics:

- Ability to Meet Market Needs and Preferences
- Costs (not price)
- Service
- Reputation
- Financial Strength
- Proprietary Position
- Market Share

Looking at each of the competitive position factors, how do you compare with the competition? Are you strong, weak, or somewhere in between?

Keeping Score

The interesting and great thing about this process is that much of the work for this part has already been done. All you have to do is go back to Chapter 9 and look at the worksheets you prepared for Figures 9-1 and 9-2. You'll see that you've already done a good bit of brainwork for plotting your segments in this chart. You just need to go back and lift it out.

So, go back and look at what you did. Analyze it and think about it in terms of the rating systems—high to low for market attractiveness and strong to weak for competitive position. Judge each of the characteristics listed and plot a point along the appropriate axis of the chart. Start by looking at your prepared sheets, but go a step beyond that information. Make your final rating a well-considered response to the question asked.

It's a judgment call. You don't have to be perfect, but you'd like to have a sufficiently accurate representation that you can feel confident about formulating a strategy.

For *market attractiveness*, you're trying to get a good read on whether an outside investor might view the segment as a good bet. For example, the average *real* growth rate in all sectors of the economy has been 3% over the past 50 years. An outsider might view a growth rate that's significantly higher than that—say 10%—as highly attractive. A growth rate of 1% or less might be viewed as less attractive.

For the *competitive position ratings*, you need to evaluate how your company stacks up against current competitors in the market segment. How do you *really* rate your quality compared with the quality of your competitors? Does your service really give you an advantage in the marketplace? To rate your position as strong, you must see strong evidence that these characteristics give you significant advantage in the market.

You can plot each of the market attractiveness factors and the competitive position factors on the strategic assessment chart as shown in Figure 13-2.

For each factor in market attractiveness, you have to look at the information developed in Chapter 9 (Figure 9-1) and judge where each item should be located along the horizontal axis from high to low. In this example, market growth and profit levels were judged moderate, while absence of threats or product displacement were considered highly attractive factors.

Competitive position ranges along the vertical axis from weak to strong. The '+,' 'OK,' and '-' ratings developed in Chapter 9 (Figure 9-2) can be used to locate points along the vertical axis.

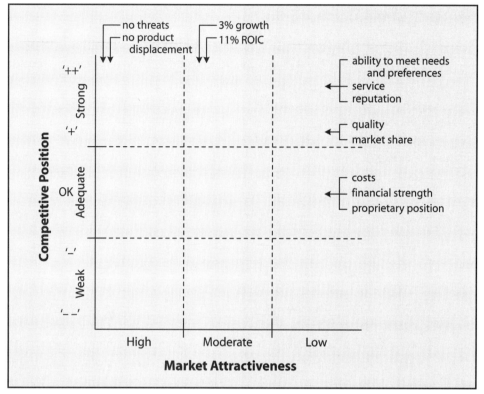

Figure 13-2. Strategic assessment chart

Strategic Assessment Matrix

This concept of plotting market attractiveness and competitive position can be formalized into a tool we call the *strategic assessment matrix*. This is a nine-box matrix that can help you analyze each of your chosen market segments. This tool will enable you to go back and look at some of the information you've researched and figure out how it fits into an assessment of your future strategies.

Think of the strategic assessment matrix (Figure 13-4) as a guide to help you chart a suggested strategy based on information you've gathered. Remember that this is merely a guide. Strategy should never be mechanistic. At some point, you have to make decisions that you trust in your gut. But here's the best strategy tool that we know of to feed into your gut. It takes into account most of the information we've been discussing.

In the strategic assessment at the top of the worksheet (Figure 13-3), look at the factors for market attractiveness and plot them along the horizontal axis of the matrix. The point that is the average of these plots on this matrix represents the market segment's attractiveness. When you plot each point, be more specific than merely "High" or "Moderate" or "Low." Find the position along the axis that most appropriately represents the value of each point.

Then, after you've plotted attractiveness on the horizontal axis, you should plot your company's competitive position. To do this, look at the factors for competitive position and plot them along the vertical axis of the same matrix. The point that is the average of these plots on the matrix represents your company's competitive position in this market segment. Again, plot your points as specifically as possible, not just as "Strong" or "Adequate" or "Weak."

Date:_____
STRATEGIC ASSESSMENT FOR: Worksheet No.: 5.1
Interior Packaging for Hard Candy

Market Attractiveness Summary	
Rate of future real industry market volume growth for our products in this market segment	3%
Average future industry profit level for our products in this market segment	11%
Major threats to market	None
Potential for product displacement	None
Competitive Position Summary	
Ability to meet market needs and preferences	++
Quality	+
Costs (not price)	OK
Service	++
Reputation	++
Financial strength	OK
Propietary position	OK
Current market share	24%
Future market share	30%

Figure 13-3. Strategic assessment worksheet

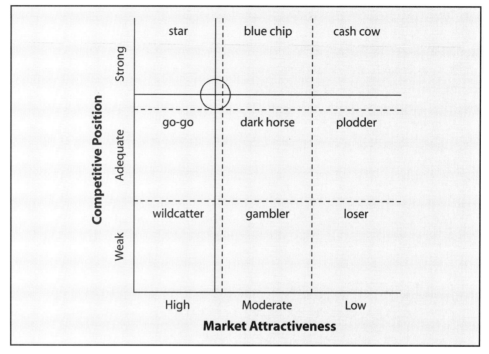

Figure 13-4. Market attractiveness/competitiveness matrix

After plotting the market attractiveness and your competitive position, you want to find where the two positions intersect. The intersection gives you an approximate location of the market segment on this matrix. You can see how this technique has been used in Figure 13-4.

In the Meeting

During the second meeting, take about 20 minutes to summarize the market attractiveness and competitive position for each market segment using Figure 13-3. Then plot the location of the segment on the matrix (Figure 13-4). It's also helpful to make a composite matrix, to show all market segments on one plot.

What It Means—Strategy

Each of your market segments will fall into one of the boxes in our matrix—star, cash cow, wildcatter, dark horse, etc. Once you've identified your current positions in the matrix, you should think about how you could influence each of those positions. It's an interesting question. You have some control over how your segments fall in this matrix. So, are you satisfied with your current standing in this market segment?

Strategic Tip

While looking at this matrix, remember that markets can become more or less attractive (horizontal position) and individual companies usually do not have any control over this. But companies have considerable control over how they stack up against the competition (vertical position).

Once you find out where you are, the question is *Where do you want to be?*

Most people think that their company should be in the upper left-hand corner. This makes a lot of sense: it's hard to argue with a strong position in a highly attractive market. This thinking suggests that you may wish to expand in segments on the left side of the matrix—you want your company to grow in the most attractive areas. But if your company is in less attractive areas, you may wish to shrink your presence or even get out altogether.

For each market segment, there are five choices:

1. **Expand:** Use aggressive posture to grow market share. The goal is for sales growth to significantly exceed market growth.
2. **Maintain**: Mount a vigorous defense of market share. This does not mean stagnate. The goal is for sales growth to at least match market growth.
3. **Contract:** Use a pruning strategy. The goal is to shrink total sales while increasing profitability.
4. **Milk:** Gently coax resources out of a business segment. This does not mean bleed. The goal is to minimize investment and maximize cash flow.
5. **Withdraw:** Exit over a brief time.

So look again at the matrix and find the position of one of your market segments—and notice the recommended *strategies for your core businesses* (Figure 13-5).

As you plot each segment using this matrix, you'll begin to see where your core businesses are positioned. But there's more to think about than just your core businesses. You're probably considering some opportunities that may fall outside your core business. How you treat these should be driven, to some extent, by where your main core business market segments lie.

| | Market Attractiveness | | |
	High	Moderate	Low
Strong	**Star** Expand core business segment	**Blue Chip** Expand or maintain core business segment	**Cash Cow** Milk, maintain, or contract core business segment
Adequate	**Go-Go** Expand core business segment	**Dark Horse** ??? core business segment	**Plodder** Milk or withdraw from core business segment
Weak	**Wildcatter** Expand core business segment	**Gambler** Expand or withdraw from core business segment	**Loser** Withdraw from core business segment

Competitive Position (vertical axis label)

Figure 13-5. Indicated market strategies for core businesses

Identify your most important core business segments and determine the average position of those segments. Locate this average position in the matrix and read the recommended strategy for *expansion outside the core business* to determine how much of an appetite you should have for opportunities outside the core business. If, for example, your most important core segments tend to be in the upper right corner around the "cash cow" position, you probably have a mature business and need to be strongly pursuing new opportunities to replace your maturing core segments.

When using these two guides, remember that the essence of strategy is deciding where to invest time and money—and, by implication, where *not* to invest. You want to invest your time and money in those areas that offer the best payback. It's not unusual for there to be competition for resources between existing segments and new opportunities. The question is how to pick the most attractive segments or opportunities for expansion. The answer is that you start deciding by looking at the matrix.

If an individual market segment falls on the left side of the matrix, it's most likely worth investing in. On the other hand, if many of your segments

		Market Attractiveness		
		High	Moderate	Low
Competitive Position	Strong	**Star** Expand outside core businesses	**Blue Chip** Expand outside core businesses	**Cash Cow** Expand outside core businesses
	Adequate	**Go-Go** Possibly expand outside core businesses	**Dark Horse** Possibly expand outside core businesses	**Plodder** Get into some other business
	Weak	**Wildcatter** Do not expand outside core businesses	**Gambler** Do not expand outside core businesses or get into some other business	**Loser** Get into some other business

Figure 13-6. Indicated market strategies for expansion outside of core businesses

fall on the left side, you'll likely have to limit yourself to one or two "expand" strategies. You'll need to *focus* your resources rather than spread them too thinly across several segments. And you may not need to invest in opportunities outside your core business in order to grow.

The market segments that fall on the right side are places to consider taking resources from in order to invest in the things on the left side of the matrix. Getting these resources may be a matter of milking the segment, contracting, or withdrawing altogether. If *many* of your segments fall on the right side, then you may have a very mature business. In this case it's prudent to be looking hard at new opportunities to complement maturing segments.

Strategy is about making choices. This matrix gives you a starting point for making those choices. It should stimulate good strategic thinking and constructive debate, but do not view it as an "automatic strategy selector." You've probably been managing your business for a while, so you should rely on a combination of analysis and experience. In the end, you still have to trust your instincts. Now that you see all of this, what do you think?

If you make a choice, you begin to focus. If you focus, you should be able to break through the barriers in your way. The goal is not to start lots of projects. The goal is finish some projects. You have to look at your available resources and try to figure out what you should do and what you should let go.

Competitive Strategy

Once you've figured out what you want to do with each of your market segments, you need to figure out how you're going to try to win in the segments

that you decide to stay in. If you have a maintain strategy, how do you plan to do that?

There are two basic questions to your competitive strategy:

- Are you going after *commodity* or *specialty* customers?
- Are you working in large, undifferentiated *mass* markets or are you going after focused, *niche* markets?

Out of those two questions comes your competitive strategy, because those two questions give you four boxes in the following matrix (Figure 13-7). For a much more extensive discussion of competitive strategy, read Michael Porter's book, *Competitive Strategy* (Free Press, 1980).

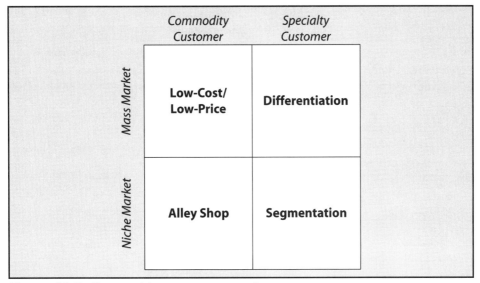

Figure 13-7. Competitive strategy matrix

As you can see, there are four possible strategies, each with a different set of features. Here are the four options:

LOW-COST/LOW-PRICE STRATEGY: Commodity strategy targeted at mass markets. This is a classic low-price strategy. The idea is to have economies of scale, no-frills product or service, and a high visibility of price. This is the type of business that has been taught in business schools for 75 years: make money with volume.

Examples:

retail:	Wal-Mart
beer:	Busch
Ford Motors:	Escort
mutual fund:	Vanguard Index 500 Fund

DIFFERENTIATION STRATEGY: Specialty strategy aimed at mass markets. This familiar American strategy is one favored by all the companies that advertise a lot. This is typically a product that conveys uniqueness and has a high degree of brand recognition; there's often a lot of advertising. Price is usually not highly visible, because the company wants you to fall in love with the features and benefits before you worry about price. A service or product positioned here does not have an outrageous price, but it costs a bit more. It has an image. This strategy has high rewards if it succeeds, but uniqueness and branding are the name of the game with this strategy—and both of these tend to require deep pockets to support these front-end costs. This strategy often gives the highest returns, but it's a high-risk game.

Examples:

retail:	Nordstrom
beer:	Budweiser
Ford Motors:	Taurus
mutual fund:	Fidelity Magellan Fund

SEGMENTATION STRATEGY: Specialty strategy aimed at niche markets. This strategy involves having specialized features aimed at a specific market segment. There may be some customization and there may even be a high visibility of price to give customers some kind of bragging rights as to how much they spent. This market tends to work with less volume but higher margins. The market is smaller, but easier to dominate if it's picked correctly.

Examples:

retail:	any corner boutique
beer:	Michelob
Ford Motors:	Lincoln
mutual fund:	Munder NetNet Fund

ALLEY SHOP STRATEGY: Commodity strategy aimed at niche markets. The only characteristic of this strategy is that things are cheap. The problem is that there's low volume and the margins on that volume are low. Though you often find companies trying this strategy, it's usually not sustainable—and certainly not a growth-oriented strategy. There's no reason to use this strategy.

No examples—bad strategy

Different competitive strategies require different skills and competencies. Let's review them briefly.

The low-cost/low-price strategy of aiming for high volume offers great rewards to the one winner (or in some rare cases two winners) that can survive the constant price wars. It requires relentless efforts to lower costs to the point that your price with an acceptable margin is below your competitor's costs. It's brutal, but the survivors can thrive. This strategy can require strong financial resources to weather years of price competition while seeking to lower costs.

The differentiation strategy typically produces a few winners in a market, but the cost and risk of creating unique products, building a brand, and advertising are very high. This strategy requires brilliant advertising and brilliant product development that create tangible differentiation that customers will value. It often also requires deep pockets, as advertising and product development are expensive and the risk of failure can be high.

The segmentation strategy can produce many winners. In fact, there can be a winner for each definable market segment. Most segments are dominated by a clear winner, then the second place position is tenable, and the rest of the market is made up of small players. The key to this strategy is understanding the unique preferences of a special group of customers and delivering them something that is "just right" for them. You need to have an intimate understanding of your customers—and you need to be nimble and flexible to follow them as their needs change.

Select a Competitive Strategy

Each market segment needs a competitive strategy. Not two, not three, but *one* competitive strategy for each segment. This is not always an easy choice. Those natural tensions in an organization rise up. Someone with a sales perspective might be attracted to the low-price strategy, where discounts make for easy sales and high volumes drive big-dollar commissions. Operations might prefer a differentiation strategy that showcases the quality and uniqueness the company can build into a product. But the financial perspective, looking at profits, could prefer to dump all of those low-margin customers and focus on the niche where the most money is made.

But wait! This isn't about individual or departmental preferences. This is about setting strategy for the company. Remember what we said in Chapter 2: you need individuals on the planning team who are able to put the interests of the company ahead of the interests of their own departments.

Each competitive strategy requires a different set of capabilities. And in most cases the capabilities and competencies you would assemble for one strategy are inappropriate or even detrimental for another strategy. For example, a low-price strategy depends on relentless attention to cost reduction. Though it's generally good to reduce costs, "relentless cost reduction" may take too much out of an offering for a specialty-niche strategy to be successful. If operations is completely focused on cost reduction (long runs to minimize changeover cost), it could be very difficult to serve the flexible requirements of the specialty-niche market that sales is targeting.

Look at the situation for each market. Map out which strategies your competitors are following. Look for ways to avoid them: for example, if there's a crowd pursuing differentiation and low-price strategies, consider a segmentation strategy. Assess what it would take to beat any competitor following your selected strategy and evaluate whether you have the capabilities and competencies to be successful. Remember: strategy is about making clear choices that will optimize your future potential. It's time to choose.

Now you know where you're going. As you continue forward, you'll learn more about how to pursue and support your chosen strategies so you actually achieve them.

chapter 14

Complete Your Vision

YOU'VE GOT A MIGHTY FINE VISION—BUT IT ISN'T FINISHED YET. There's more to it. Although you've mostly figured out your core business strategies by now, there are things outside your core business to consider. There are opportunities— opportunities that you've thought about but that you must now narrow to the few that fit with your strategy and are doable. And you need to figure out whether your competencies match up with your vision. Do you envision pursuing what you're best at? Finally, what capabilities are necessary for a company that intends to pull off a vision such as yours?

As you begin to complete your vision, you will see how it all fits together. Strategy is *complex* because there are a lot of elements. But it doesn't have to be *complicated* in order to be *complete*. When you start to see the elements weave together to become a tapestry, it's a beautiful thing.

Targeting Strategic Opportunities

Earlier you spent some time looking at a variety of possible new directions. You now want to decide which ones make sense, to decide which opportunities (outside your core business) you're going to commit to during the next three to five years.

So, look at the opportunities that passed your screens back in Chapter 10. Some are intended for your core segments; you should consider including those in your core segment strategies. The rest will be outside your core business. It's time to narrow these down to *no more than* three or four workable ideas. The number depends on the resources available and on the magnitude of the new undertakings.

There are different ways to sort out which new ideas make sense. While *every* company will have its own set of factors with differing levels of importance, there are a few things all companies should consider.

One of the first key things to consider is the strategic focus that you defined back in Chapter 12. If you've listed some ideas that fall outside your stated focus, you should eliminate them—or *carefully* consider changing your focus.

Another thing to take into account is the overall capacity of the organization. Look back at the market segment strategies you identified in Chapter 13. If you have several market segments that you plan to expand or maintain, and there's a vigorous demand on resources from your core business, you probably want to strongly limit the new opportunities to which you'll be committing. On the other hand, if you have a mature core business that's about to give out on you as the market matures and flattens out, it's probably imperative for you to start pursuing new opportunities.

But you have to consider the magnitude of the idea and what resources it will take to pull it off. If each of your opportunities is big—things like *Enter the Chinese market* or

---

Strategic Tip

Opportunities are more than just tactics. Keep your opportunity list short and significant. Improving delivery time on janitorial supplies or buying new dictionaries are not the kind of opportunities that should be considered in most industries. Instead, concentrate on adding new products or new markets or on making a major operating improvement, such as a new factory or new distribution channel. Doing a few things well is much better than starting many things and finishing nothing.

In the Meeting

During the second meeting, you need to narrow your list of opportunities to those that make sense for your company. If there's no clear consensus in this matter, then there may be a strategic issue that should be captured (on the worksheet in Figure 12-1) and discussed. You want to agree on the few opportunities outside the core business that you'll commit to achieving during the three- to five-year strategic time frame.

Introduce entirely redesigned product line or *Build a new plant*—they will require a lot of resources. If your ideas are a little smaller—*Extend the product life with an incremental improvement*—you can do more of those.

Choosing and Enhancing Strategic Competencies

So you now have a core business strategy made up of a set of market segments, each with a clear strategy (expand, maintain, and so forth). You have a focus. You've established a set of opportunities that you intend to pursue. Now it's time to figure out a way to support your strategy. What skills and know-how will it take to accomplish all of these things?

General Fasteners is a distributor that sells nuts, bolts, rivets, and any other mechanical fasteners. The problem confronting the managers of General Fasteners when they first tried to find a strategic competency is the basic fact that a bolt is a bolt. They're all pretty much the same. Thus, the managers really had to reach to find a way to be different.

> ### Tales from the Strategy Vault
> Walt Disney is an example of a company that started with one strategic competency—animated movies—and, while maintaining that competency, has grown into a far broader competency—family entertainment. This includes television, theme parks, movies (both animated and live), books, resorts, real estate, stores, and a cruise line. In each area where Disney makes great profits, the competency of family entertainment creates tremendous value for customers.

They began looking at what customers really wanted and they discovered that customers didn't want to run out of nuts and bolts when a production line was running. So General Fasteners developed a "Fastener Management Program," which was a contract that provided for General Fasteners employees to provide many production management tools and even bin stocking in their customers' plants. They began doing things that the customers previously had done themselves. They turned doing everything for a customer with regard to fasteners into their competency. It was brilliant. And although that strategy would at first glance appear to be easy to copy, the company developed it to the point that it could quickly set up warehouses of fasteners near big customers, no matter where they were. General Fasteners used its competency and then was ready to make changes when necessary.

That's the idea of a strategic competency. Don't just be good. Be world-class. Find something and go all out. Pick a place to win and then go ahead and win. You don't need a million strategic competencies. You don't want a million of them. Pick one or two specific things and concentrate.

A key point: in order to succeed with a strategic competency, you can't just be good at it. The competency must really make your company *stand out*. Companies that have outstanding competencies tend to have very successful strategies. What are the two or three strategic competencies you intend to build up to world-class capability?

Take a look back at those current strategic competencies you identified in Chapter 7. Are those the right ones? Are they enough to support your strategic vision? If so, then it all fits together: the tapestry begins to take shape. If not, then you need to figure what competencies you need to build in order to make the strategy work. Remember, strategic competencies are:

- Valuable to the customer
- Different from the competition
- Difficult to copy

These competencies should be your most important source of competitive advantage and they're most powerful when they're consistent with your strategic focus.

Competencies are not easy to build. Building a world-class strategic competency can take most of your resources for five to 10 years. If you're thinking about building new competencies, you should not even consider building more than one at a time.

Once you've identified your desired strategic competencies, they will become the focal point for hiring, training, and corporate development efforts.

> ### In the Meeting
>
> During the second meeting, selecting your future strategic competencies is a strategic issue. (Include it in the worksheet in Figure 12-1.) Discuss your current strategic competencies, your strategic focus, and other elements of your emerging strategy to determine no more than three strategic competencies you will commit to building to world-class status in the next five to 10 years.

Choosing and Enhancing Capabilities

What do you need to be *able* to do in order to execute the strategy? Beyond strategic competencies, there are systems and internal capabilities that you need to have in order to pull off your vision as stated so far.

A good place to start is with your list of strengths and weaknesses (in Chapter 6). Are there any weaknesses that you need to consider? As we said before, you don't want to dwell on the negative, but you may want to consider critical weaknesses that could derail you and then develop a strategy to avoid or fix them.

How about opportunities? Sometimes, there are tactical or minor strategic opportunities in the operations of a company that stimulate thought about which capabilities to build.

In addition, look at your winner's profile from Chapter 11 and consider which capabilities you need to build in order to become such a winner.

There are certain capabilities that, if enhanced, will give you strategic benefit. Those are the ones to concentrate on. If a capability enables you to be more effective with your strategies, than you should pay attention to it. But not all capabilities are important. For example, you may have a capability of having really clean windows in your office, but that doesn't give strategic benefit unless the appearance of your windows is somehow important to your customer. For instance, this could be an important capability for a window cleaning company.

> ### In the Meeting
> During the second meeting, as part of the strategic issues exercise (Worksheet 12-1), discuss and identify a short list of critical capabilities that need to be in place to support the emerging vision of your company.

So how many capabilities should you concentrate on? Probably about a half dozen, certainly not more than a dozen. The important point is that they be critical things that build on your strategy.

Pay Attention to Corporate Culture

When businesspeople talk about strategy, often they talk about the "hard" side of strategy—the market and competitive aspects. The concentration is usually on the quantitative and analytical. But there's another, equally important side, a softer side.

It's important that your culture be aligned with your strategy, because one of the critical things in any company is the motivation of employees. In other words, why do your employees do things?

There are two related questions. What do you want the experience of working for your company to be like? And what do you want the experience of dealing with your company to be like for a customer? These two things must be aligned with your strategy.

Culture is important to your strategy in many ways. Your strategy will dictate what kind of workers you want. For instance, a company that has a strategy of building its source of advantage into its systems may depend less on the skill and experience level of its employees. It may be able to have a corporate culture that is built around hiring young employees and keeping them for a year or two at most.

On the other hand, if you require expertise and experience to execute your strategy, you probably want to build a culture to attract and retain people who fit your vision.

A good example of a company that must consider culture is one that's growing fast. In one such company that we know, the managers knew that rapid growth would require loyal workers who would be flexible enough to evolve into new jobs as the company grew. So, they spent time thinking about ways to encourage people to stay and, in fact, bring in friends and family to work there. This was a company that would have a strong demand for workers in the next few years and they decided the best way to look for them was through people who were already working there.

> **Tales from the Strategy Vault**
>
> In the McDonald's food chain, there's a lot of turnover for employees yet not for managers. The company has a strategy of investing in systems and managers to ensure that the relatively unskilled workers follow those systems. It costs the company far less to hire and train a cook than to hire and train a manager. So the company gears its culture to encouraging young employees to use McDonald's as a steppingstone while making it desirable for managers to stay.

Use Your Brainpower

Brainpower can and should be managed and it should relate to your overall strategy. For instance, two very successful companies in the restaurant business have two different approaches. Each works because it fits with the company strategy.

McDonald's spends its money up front designing quick, efficient training for employees. They try to be effective without spending a lot of money per employee. The traditional assumption in the fast food business has been that employee turnover is chronically high, so McDonald's has applied brainpower to solving this problem. Over the past 20 years, McDonald's has optimized efficiency by designing both its operations and its training process to turn *new* employees into *productive* employees as quickly and cheaply as possible. Interestingly, the required consistency of operations creates a value for McDonald's target markets, by ensuring a consistent product and service level in any McDonald's store.

> ### Tales from the Strategy Vault
>
> Many companies will have a strategic issue around the topic of organizational design, culture, or motivation of employees. If any of these come up, discuss them and capture the resulting vision as part of the strategic issues exercise (Worksheet 12-1).

On the other hand, Outback Steakhouse has *every* new employee spend quite a bit of time on training, and their costs per employee are high. Outback has applied their brainpower in a very different way. Instead of trying to succeed by making turnover less costly, they have made it more costly—but they have also lowered their turnover rate. In part, this is accomplished by giving the employees a "piece of the action." In addition, Outback spends more on training per employee than any other national restaurant chain. Both of these policies increase costs, but they lower turnover and improve motivation. Outback uses the superior training, motivation, and lower turnover to improve the value of the service to the customer. Outback offers a more friendly, personalized service that their more upscale customers value highly and the company can deliver this increased value because they spend more on developing their employees.

Both McDonald's and Outback understand that brainpower in the service industry is important, but they harness it in different ways. And those ways of applying brainpower automatically make their service offerings much more attractive to different segments of the restaurant market.

Align Your Money with Your Strategy

Just as you need a culture that's well aligned with your strategy, so too you need to at least consider aligning your financial approach with your strategy.

Of course, not *every* company has or needs a vision about its financial position. There are many companies that are successful without explicitly defining their vision of their financial approach. If you feel comfortable not having a financial strategy, it's OK not to have one.

However, there are circumstances that would make it worthwhile to consider such issues. For instance, if you're about to undergo a period of rapid growth, you may want to consider becoming a publicly traded company. You may simply want to develop your banking relationships in order to get some working capital. In addition, if you intend to make some major acquisitions, you probably want to reduce your debt load so you can go to banks for bridge financing.

> **In the Meeting**
>
> If issues of financial strategy arise, discuss them and capture the resulting vision as part of the strategic issues exercise (worksheet 12-1).

How Big Do You Want to Be?

So what's your intention? Look over everything you've done up to here and figure out where this is taking you. If you have this focus, if you expand some markets and maintain others, if you pursue the opportunities you've chosen, where will it all lead? In three to five years, if you're allowed three sentences in *The Wall Street Journal* to describe your company, what will they be?

> **In the Meeting**
>
> As you work through the key elements of creating a strategy, it's important to pause and distill it back down to its essence. Without worrying about wording, get the team to summarize the intention for growth and size in a few sentences.

How Many Ways Can You Shoot Yourself in the Foot?

At this point, the strategic issue discussions should have resolved the key elements of your strategy. A clear, though preliminary vision of where you intend to take the company over the next three to five years should be emerging. Before you finalize all these great plans of yours, step back and think about unexpected consequences. What could go wrong?

For example, if there was a decision to exit a particular market, think about unexpected consequences. Could it hurt sales in another market you want to maintain, because you didn't realize there was synergy between the two markets?

If there was a decision to change your suppliers to lower your costs, could there be potential of losing quality because of that?

As we said before, you don't want to dwell on the negative. But you don't want to be caught by surprise either.

Remember, there are down sides to almost any good idea. In fact, anything you're thinking of doing probably has unintended consequences. They may be good, but they also may be bad. The idea is not to freeze up with worry but rather to become aware of the possibilities and think about steps to take to reduce the impact of possible bad consequences. The question is, how bad can it get—and are you willing to take that on?

> ### Tales from the Strategy Vault
>
> A manufacturer of truck components we know wanted to get into a new product line, but needed one part that was very expensive to manufacture in their plant. So they decided to find a lower-cost source for that component. They found a supplier that had very high quality, well-trained workers, and a great record on delivery. As a bonus, they were easy to work with. Confident that their new vendor would allow their product to be successful, they went out and signed up many new customers for the product at a very competitive price. Unfortunately, the new supplier was located in a little country that used to be known as Yugoslavia. When civil war broke out, an embargo was imposed and there was no way to get the component. Suddenly, they couldn't meet their commitments to their new customers. A good idea had backfired; they had shot themselves in the foot.

Put It Down on Paper

Now it's time to put it all down in writing so you can see what you've decided. Write down in short, succinct form your sense of course and direction. Once again:

> ### In the Meeting
>
> Look back over the tentative strategy developed in the strategic issue discussions. For each 'good idea' ask about any unexpected consequences and list them as shown in the worksheet, Figure 14-1. Do not spend a lot of time on this. Cover it and move on. A half-hour is plenty in most cases. If any major vulnerabilities are identified, you can modify your vision when you finalize your strategies.

HOW MANY WAYS COULD WE SHOOT OURSELVES IN THE FOOT?

Date:_____
Worksheet No.: 5.3

Good Idea	Unexpected Consequence
Buy from new, low-price supplier	Supplier cannot deliver product on time
Push for rapid growth	Grow beyond resource capacity
Promote from within	Go beyond people's level of competence
Push to develop attractive new growth opportunities for near-term profits	Accept down-side risks that we should not due to insufficient investigation
Lean and mean staffing	Weak or no backup for managers
Rapid introduction of new products	Untested product fails or underperforms
Save money on operations	Poor service due to inadequate systems

Figure 14-1. The "how many ways could we shoot ourselves in the foot?" worksheet

- What is your strategic focus?
- What is your market strategy in each segment?
- What is your competitive strategy in each segment?
- What opportunities will you pursue?
- What strategic competencies do you need?
- What capabilities should you develop?
- What is your intention regarding your size?

In the Meeting

Take about two to three hours in the second meeting to write down your sense of vision as to the course and direction of the enterprise, following the format in the worksheet in Figure 14-2.

If you've done a good job of discussing and resolving each strategic issue, it should not take long to outline your strategies in a format that will serve as a key guide to the management team.

STRATEGIES	Date:_____
	Worksheet No.: 5.4-1

Management's sense of vision as to the intended course and direction of the enterprise

A. Strategic Focus:
Product line: Interior and exterior packaging

B. Core Business Strategies
1. ***Interior Packaging for Hard Candy***
Market Strategy: Maintain
- Match Brown advertising campaign.
- Launch two new products each year.
- Maintain control of high-profile Jones account.

Competitive Strategy: Specialty/Niche Market
- Improve cycle time on quotes.
- Excellent color match.
- Implement a premier account program.

2. ***Interior Packaging for Soft Candy***
Market Strategy: Expand
- Launch one market leadership product each year.
- Add applications engineers to support sales effort.
- Get 100% of business at Harbor Gourmet Candy.

Competitive Strategy: Specialty/Niche Market
- Monitor National for indicators of entry into the specialty market.
- Resist taking commodity business at Acme Sweets.
- Value-based pricing: test prices upward constantly.

3. ***Interior Packaging for Bakery***
Market Strategy: Maintain
- Launch one new product each year.
- Shore up sales force in Chicago with new sales rep.

Competitive Strategy: Commodity/Mass Market
- Obtain more competitive materials costs.

4. ***Exterior Packaging for Candy, Bakery, and Miscellaneous Dry Packaged Foods***
Market Strategy: Expand
- Focus on accounts that need four-color short-run packaging.
- Develop new advertising campaign and sales literature.

Competitive Strategy: Specialty/Niche Market
- Obtain Bobst die cutter.

Figure 14-2. Strategies

- Focus on accounts with potential of $50,000+ per year.
- Be at forefront of industry technology.
- Improve knowledge of market price tolerance.
- Ensure fast response to customers.

C. Opportunities/Initiatives Outside the Core Business
New Products
- Obtain entry in non-food interior packaging. This product line must have a low front-end cost for both tooling and marketing. Use existing tooling where possible. Must be market that values our hygienic capability and other competencies to provide specialty status.
- Develop Tek-pak.

New Markets
- Investigate entry in Canadian market.

D. Strategic Competencies
- Interior packaging design expertise.
- Cost-effective manufacturing.
- Exterior packaging appearance.
- Plastics packaging expertise.

E. Internal Development
Enhancements to Strategic Competencies
- Send each exterior package designer to graphic arts course.
- Implement lower-cost flexible manufacturing process.

Corporate Capabilities
- Achieve shortest new product development cycle among competitors (Worksheet No. 1.2).
- Maintain technical leadership by recruiting the best engineers.
- Install MIS upgrade.
- Develop product line costing system.
- Achieve ISO 9000 certification.

Organizational Strategies
- Develop and empower second tier of management.

Financial/Ownership Strategies
- Reduce long-term debt by at least 50%.
- Investigate public offering.

F. Growth/Size
- Largest supplier in Midwest.
- Grow sales and profits at 10%-15%/year (double every 5-7 years).

Figure 14-2. (continued)

There it is. You have a strategy for your company! Whew, it really wasn't so bad after all.

But that isn't the end of the story. The vision is nice, but we need to translate that vision into commitments if we hope to get results. And results, after all, are what we want.

chapter 15

Support Strategy with Commitments

STRATEGY IS MORE THAN JUST GOOD IDEAS. You actually have to do something in order to bring about some results. At some point you must translate your nice words on paper into tangible things that *you can do*.

You started with the vision. After all, strategy is about vision. But success doesn't happen just because you think of a vision. Articulating the vision is a step. But to make the vision work, you have to narrow it into workable chunks for actual human beings to grasp and accomplish. There are some steps requiring planning between strategy and action (Figure 15-1).

The Mission Statement as Foundation

Hey, this is what this company is about.

It's interesting. Most people who want to do strategy think you should start with a mission statement, because they think that you can somehow decide the biggest of your big pictures without understanding any of the details. Hogwash! Start instead with some details so you know what you're talking about.

We recommend you wait until this point to write a mission statement, for many reasons. One key reason is because many of the elements of a good

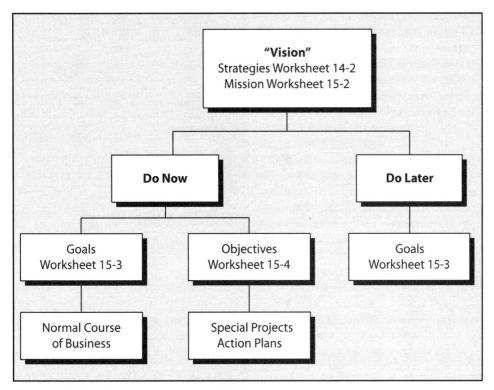

Figure 15-1. Vision is expressed in the strategy and mission statement. Goals and objectives are statements of what we have to do to achieve that vision.

mission statement come right from your strategy. The two overlap considerably, and you can find specific things in your strategy to put into your mission statement.

One big difference between your strategy and your mission statement is that the mission statement is so *public*. People see a mission statement, so there will be some areas where you'll be deliberately more vague. For instance, in a strategy you might say you plan to hit ABC

Strategic Tip

There's a reason to wait before you write your mission statement. When a company tries to write a mission statement at the beginning of the strategy process, two things can happen. One outcome could be an endless discussion. The other possibility could be worse—a generic mission statement like we showed in Chapter 3.

Company between the eyes and take all their business away. You may not

Tales from the Strategy Vault

In the 1960s, many people were aware that part of the Disney mission was to grow its theme park business. What was not in the mission statement but was in the strategy was the intention to open a theme park in central Florida. If that information had been public, real estate prices in that area would have shot up, making such a huge undertaking nearly impossible. Instead, Disney set up hundreds of small companies that went about quietly purchasing land in central Florida.

Tales from the Strategy Vault

Southwest Airlines is completely obsessed with providing the cheapest seat from Point A to Point B. And that's it. So, they have essentially decided to provide the best of anything they can provide for free. Therefore, the low-cost airline has a very friendly staff. But food is optional on a plane, so they provide almost no food—just peanuts.

be that blunt in your mission statement. Instead, you may say you want to seek growth in a market that happens to contain ABC Company.

The other important thing to consider about the public nature of a mission statement is its symbolic value. It really is a declaration. You define who you are and why your customers, employees, and community support your existence. Part of that declaration—maybe the most important part—is when you declare what you *will not do*. Although mission statements are seldom explicit about what a company doesn't do, you should nevertheless draw clear lines.

So, what goes into a good mission statement? At this stage, you need ideas, not perfect grammar or punctuation. You don't even need sentences. You need clear thoughts. If you declare three basic things, you have a *useful* mission statement:

- **Corporate Commitment**. What are your corporate commitments? Are you committed to the community? Are you committed to employees? To the environment? Are you committed to a particular technology or to brick and mortar? Some companies are and some are not. It's a simple thing to declare. What are your *real* commitments?
- **Focus**. What will you do? What will you not do? Declare it. You can express it in many forms—markets, products, needs you satisfy. Pick the description that best describes your company.
- **Identity**. This may be the slogan. You can spend time arguing words here, because this is what captures people's hearts. For instance, at Ford, "Quality is Job One" works internally and externally. The best statements of identity are the kinds that help employees and customers.

This should not take long. If you take more than a half-hour writing your mission statement, you probably don't have everyone on board and in synch with your strategy. As you'll see in more detail later, you should reexamine your mission statement annually. During the first year, you can figure out how to get people to share the mission. To demonstrate the importance of the mission statement to your company, and to give it "teeth," the person who must drive this process is the *CEO*.

A good mission statement articulates the vision to a broad public, both inside and outside the firm. But we need more than articulation of vision if we want results.

> ### Strategic Tip
>
> Don't spend time in the planning meeting choosing words or arguing over punctuation of the mission statement. A small group can easily do all that after the meetings. Also, don't be in a rush to publish your mission statement. Once published, missions are very difficult to retract. So use the outline format generated in the meeting and live it for several months or a year. Be sure the company is meeting its commitments, fulfilling its identity, and living within the focus so that it will not evoke snickers of disbelief when you go public with your statement.

Goals as a Guide to the Future

The mission statement as a declaration is a great communications tool, but real accomplishment comes from specifics. And before you begin to think about attempting new projects, you have to consistently take care of certain things. These are your goals—the stuff you have to do consistently on an ongoing basis.

> ### In the Meeting
>
> During the second meeting, discuss with your team the mission of the company. Allocate about 30-60 minutes to this discussion. Identify the commitments that your company will make. Also determine the corporate identity: what do you want people to think when they hear your company name? Then use the strategy page as a guide to develop the other elements of the mission statement, as shown in Figure 15-2.

- Goals define the routine, the day-to-day business.
- Goals are the statements of continuing intended results that are both necessary and sufficient to your concept of success.

For instance, a common goal is profitability, because this is something

---

MISSION STATEMENT   Date: _____
                                            Worksheet No.: 6.1

Corporate Commitment:
- customers
- continuous improvement
- specialty status
- ethics
- employees
- stockholders
- fun
- technical leadership

Strategic Competencies:
1. interior packaging expertise
2. cost-effective manufacturing
3. exterior packaging appearance
4. plastics packaging expertise

Strategic Focus:
- product line

Market Needs to Be Served:
1. product protection during shipment and storage
2. product appearance enhancement

Products/Services to Be Provided:
- interior and exterior protective packaging

Markets to Be Served:
- Midwest U.S. and Canadian confectioners, bakers, and other dry food processors

Market Identity:
1. most dependable/responsive supplier of interior protective packaging
2. technical expertise
3. superior value

Figure 15-2. The mission statement

you routinely want to have. Profitability is better when it's consistent and ongoing than if it's a one-time thing. If your company is like most, you want profits this year, next year, and every year after that.

A goal is something that you want to achieve every year. You don't say, "We got some profits last year so we don't need any this year." That doesn't make sense. Profits are a constant goal.

The idea of a list of goals is to identify the *five to ten things* you have to do constantly this year and every year to keep the business running. You can state your goals qualitatively, but we recommend being as quantitative as possible. However you state your goals, they must be the things that are necessary for success.

Keep the list as short as possible. We recommend the following generic list of goals to consider as a starting point:

> ### Strategic Tip
> A company would not set a goal of starting a new benefits plan, because once that's done the goal has been met. However, it could set a goal of satisfying employees—and a new benefits plan could certainly support such a goal.

- profitability
- a happy, motivated workforce
- customer satisfaction
- internal efficiency
- competitive costs
- strong financial position
- dominate a particular market
- quality
- learning and innovation

Your list can be shorter or longer, and these are only areas that we recommend considering. Every company is different, and some will find other things they need from year to year to be successful.

The more you can quantify things and write down exactly what you expect, the more your goals take real shape. You don't want them to be amorphous. You want tangible goals, so you set targets. The targets should be consistent with your strategies. Goals take the notion of vision, which you articulated in your strategy, and then orient it toward results. The key, again, is to somehow give meaning to goals. Often, this means quantifying.

> ### Strategic Tip
> When setting goals, be sure to cover the bases. Don't have all financial goals. For more ideas on how to develop nonfinancial goals, read *The Balanced Scorecard* by Robert Kaplan and David Norton (Harvard Business School Press, 1996). Go back and consider the tension triangle in Chapter 2. It's good to have at least a few goals from each perspective, as we suggested with Measures of Success in Chapter 6.

With quantifiable goals, the idea is to look about five years down the road and figure out what target makes sense for your strategy. For some companies, this means looking forward to being one number five years down the road. For others, this means looking at one number or percentage that it will meet constantly in each of the five years.

Such a set of goals will establish a balanced set of criteria for managers to strive to measure themselves against as they take care of the large portion of the business that can be

GOALS

Date:_____
Worksheet No.: 6.2

- Motivated, educated, productive, and healthy team with high levels of personal growth, pride, and satisfaction
- Total customer satisfaction
- Competitive costs
- Strong position in emerging materials technology

	2001	2002	2003	2004	2005
Financial					
Sales in $	14,800M	17,000M	20,000M	24,000M	28,000M
Operating Profit (EBIT)	>20%	>20%	>20%	>20%	>20%
Cash Flow Generated ($)	500M				1,000M
Current Assets/Current Liabilities	>200%	>200%	>200%	>200%	>200%
Customer					
Number of Customers	175	185	190	195	200
Delivery Time (avg. days)	12	12	12	7	7
% Complete on Time		>90%			>95%
Market Share in Confectionery Mkt.	>30%	>30%	>30%	>30%	>30%
Internal					
Sales/Employee ($000)	980	990	1,000	1,000	1,000
Cycle Time (days)	24	20	14	<10	<10
Scrap Rate	<1%	<1%	<1%	<1%	<1%
Innovation/Learning					
% of Sales from Products < 5 Years Old	15%				25%
Training Hours/Employee/Year	25	25	30	30	40

Figure 15-3. Goals worksheet

considered "routine." But while goals guide the ongoing incremental progress of a business, getting to "the next level" usually needs something more—it takes a project with a specific objective.

Objectives—Measurable and Specific Projects

In the end, it comes down to doing something specific. It's really simple: when you get projects finished, the company moves forward.

You can follow this from strategy to mission statement and on to goals. It really all fits together. But now is the time to figure out what it means in terms of implementation. What are you going to do? There are certain high-priority projects that you need to undertake in order to drive the company forward in the next 12 to 18 months.

The list should be short: we strongly recommend fewer than 10.

And so here you are—at the key point of the process.

This is where it happens. Suddenly, you really can turn the ideas in your strategies into action. You do it through objectives and action plans. (More later on action plans.)

We've found that if you tell a group of managers that they can set up a limited number of objectives, they will size up the objectives, their time, and other resources required to get the most from what they have. The challenge is to limit themselves to 10 objectives, because most managers think they can do everything.

The conversation about the future has already been framed at this point. So here's the question: What are the big things you can do in the next year or so to start you on the path to where you want to be in five years?

> ### Strategic Tip
>
> Based on our experience with thousands of strategic objectives, it's better to identify 10 projects and complete them all than to identify 30 projects and merely get them all started. On average, if you set 10 objectives, you should expect to complete eight or nine of them. If you set 15, you may finish seven. And if you set 20, you'll be lucky to complete two of your objectives. Once you get past 10 projects per year, you end up with diminishing returns.

Name Your Results

Objectives should be stated as results.

Objectives are not activities. Rather, objectives are statements of what you want to accomplish. Because you want to accomplish something, your objective must be specific. For instance, an objective stated as *Clean up plant* is merely an action. As a measurable objective, it means absolutely nothing. It's too general. How will you be able to tell when it's done? Are you going to paint? Do you want to gut the building and start over? It's entirely possible for a team of managers to interpret a general objective as meaning many different things. Objectives must be stated as specific expected results so that you minimize weasel room. The objective should ideally contain measurements, which must be quantitative, and be timely. In other words, you have to declare what you will do and when you are going to do it—specifically.

When you measure something, you put a psychological degree of importance on it for all of your workers. For example, we once had a client who was very focused on growth; everyone in the company knew what his growth target was—25%. He was growing at 25% a year but, when he came to us, he couldn't figure out why all this growth wasn't translating into profits. And the answer, of course, is that no one in the company knew that profits were important, but they sure understood how their roles in the company related to growth. His only focus was growth, and he was successful at that because he was aiming for it.

> ## Tales from the Strategy Vault
>
> In the early years of Ben & Jerry's Ice Cream, a plant manager purchased an ice cream packing machine for about $20,000. This was an expensive piece of equipment, back when a good car cost $10,000. At the time, one of the owners, Ben Cohen, was skeptical about the purchase. How could a machine be worth that much money? Well, the plant manager explained that the machine could pack 2,000 pints of ice cream an hour without hiring any new employees. They gave it a try, but Ben stipulated that the machine would be sold if it didn't reach that output. So they put up a big piece of plywood on the wall, painted a 'goal line,' and then charted the results. Funny thing: once the line reached 2,000 pints an hour, it just kept going up. Pretty soon, they were doing 4,000 pints an hour. The employees clearly *saw* that the output was being measured, so they pushed it because it was deemed important. Measurement creates results.

Go for an Easy Win First

Nothing helps like confidence. And nothing builds confidence better than a legitimate reason to puff out your chest. It helps to win.

If you know when you set out to do a project that you will succeed, it makes it easier to do the project. So we recommend in the early stages of the strategy process that you find some doable, specific projects. You don't want anything *too* easy, because you want to be able to feel a sense of accomplishment, but you don't want a bunch of huge projects that will overwhelm you. Balance is important.

Some companies are successful with only two projects a year. Some can do only one and some can do three. It depends on the scope. But it's important to recognize that if you try to take on five gargantuan projects in one year you'll be unable to succeed at them. This will lead to a feeling of failure that can be associated with your planning process in the minds of the participants.

The first year, in particular, we recommend you create some bite-sized chunks to take on. This will give the team a chance to feel good about your company's progress. Projects are even better if they're public— something like purchasing and installing a new phone system that's customer-friendly. If your phone system is annoying customers and preventing you from delivering good service, then correcting this problem will have immediate benefit to the business and serve as a highly visible sign that planning can lead to results.

In the Meeting
At the end of the second meeting, you need to set objectives to drive your strategy. To do this thoughtfully will take you one to two hours. Ask your team members to look back at the strategy, mission, and goals worksheets, and each identify what he or she thinks are the most important projects to move the company toward success.
To get balanced input, give each team member a chance to propose his or her top-priority objective. (If another member has mentioned that objective, take a lower-priority objective.) Add to the list until about 12-15 objectives have been identified, then ask the team to assign each a priority rating, as shown on the worksheet in Figure 15-4.
Review the objectives and ratings and cut the list to fewer than 10 objectives. Assign a leader and a backup to write the action plan for each objective and manage its accomplishment over the next 12-18 months.

Your employees will start to look at all projects and think, "We can do this!"

OBJECTIVES

Date: _____
Worksheet No.: 6.3

Objective Number	Priority	Objective	Action Plan Team Leader
3	1	Have new computer system on line by / / .	RPB/HLR
5	1	Begin EDI processing with both Acme and Jones by / / .	RPB/BKS
1	2	Achieve meaningful employee motivation by establishing a new participative management and incentive program and motivate all employees to achieve at least 5% bonus by / / .	GFM/HLR
4	3	Spruce up and maintain plant and office by / / .	JCB/CSS
8	3	Develop an integrated sales management plan and achieve $1,000,000 in non-food interior packaging sales by / / .	SDD/HLR
6	5	Reduce costs 2% through establishment of a cost control process by / / .	NSH/BKS
7	5	Launch new advertising campaign with completely new sales materials for Exterior Packaging for Candy, Bakery, and Miscellaneous Dry Packaged Foods by / / .	SDD/JCB
9	6	Acquire specialty packaging manufacturer with plastics packaging expertise by / / .	NSH/SDD
2	7	Complete cross training of all first-line manufacturing personnel by / / .	GFM/CSS
10	7	Make a decision on the Canadian market by / / .	SDD/NSH

Figure 15-4. Developing objectives worksheet

Identifying and assigning objectives completes the three-day strategy formulation meeting (second meeting). It's now time to take a break from the meetings and do some off-line preparation for implementation: develop action plans, budgets, and time planning. Each of these is covered in the next two chapters. You should review these with your team and assign the tasks as required in preparation for the final implementation-planning meeting.

Part Five

Create a Way to Get Things Done

EVEN SPECIFIC WORDS DON'T GET MUCH DONE unless those words drive to some form of clear accountability. Now it's time to put it all together into a cohesive group of action plans that translate the grand vision of your strategy into a detailed set of tasks with people, resources, and a schedule attached. In the next three chapters, you'll learn how to write action plans, honestly evaluate resources required, and set realistic schedules that people buy into without the usual problems of "sandbagging" or overcommitment.

Finally, you'll see how simplified strategic planning really works. With the planning done, we'll leave you with a monitoring program to ensure that you achieve your desired results. You have to check in on the plans once in a while. You must be accountable and willing to learn from the process. And you learn as you go. Every plan gets better, because this is not a one-time Soviet-style five-year plan you're doing here. It's a process, not an event. It works because it starts and ends in reality. And you learn because it's recursive—each time you get better at everything.

So what are you waiting for? This is not the time to stop! This is the point where you turn your intentions into results and make it all come together. Turn the page—you're into the home stretch.

chapter 16

Write an Action Plan

T HE IDEA OF STRATEGY IS NOT TO MERELY WRITE A STORY ABOUT SUCCESS. It's to actually succeed. So, you need to do something specific, you need to assign someone to do it in a specific amount of time, and you need to pay for it. You need an action plan.

An action plan is the main driver of results, the roadmap that allows you to achieve your objectives.

It's relatively easy to describe objectives. The test of a successful strategy is converting those objectives into results. That's where action plans come in. Action plans translate the grand strategic objectives into a series of specific, bite-sized, doable actions with human and financial resources allocated to ensure success. The beauty of this process is that, if you do it right, you will know who is supposed to do what and when.

The beauty is in the sequence: the entire simplified process is easy to follow when it's in a step-by-step format. Strategic planning is a process of going from the general to the specific—and at this point of the process you're committing to some very specific things.

Why Bother with Action Plans?

You have the vision. What more do you need?

We've found that a common problem with other approaches to strategy is that many stop with goals and objectives. They figure that if you have some objectives, someone will figure out how to get them done. In most companies, however, things don't get done: they get buried in the noise of day-to-day business.

> **Tales from the Strategy Vault**
>
> Our experience backs up the research showing that when American businesses set objectives of any sort (e.g., quality, financial, strategic, operational) they generally achieve only about a third of them. We set out to change this. Adding action plans to the simplified strategic planning process raised the typical accomplishment rate to 50% to 60%. Then we went on to add other implementation tools (which we'll explain in the coming chapters). If you closely follow the process laid out in this book, your company should achieve 80% to 90% of your chosen strategic objectives within one or two months of your scheduled deadlines.

We've noticed that unless companies have a specific programmed commitment to do some very specific things in an action plan, those things will simply get deferred. And then years go by and nothing happens. But if you take the time to break projects into reasonable chunks, allocate the time and money necessary for each step, and develop a schedule to complete each task, you have a good chance of seeing them turn into reality. Without this, objectives are merely a wish list.

Who Writes It?

It starts with a leader and a backup leader, two members of the strategic planning team who were drafted at the middle planning meeting when you chose the objective. These two people have primary responsibility for drafting the action plan. But since they do so outside the meeting, it's to their advantage to get help from two or three others who may be involved in executing the action plan. Getting broad buy-in early in the process helps ensure successful execution of action plans. After these members of the team write the plan, the entire strategy team reviews it and approves it.

Filling Out the Form

We've developed a unique, easy-to-understand, and proven template for writing action plans. Our action plan is not just a list of things to do, but rather a comprehensive tool that includes sequential flow of tasks, resource allocation, and scheduled commitments. Both time and money are allocated very specifically, so that everyone can follow every step and know how much of each is required for each step.

The Basic Elements

An action plan should be a simple roadmap that leads to the accomplishment of an objective. Each objective will have an action plan: if you have eight objectives, you will have eight action plans.

Each action plan is usually one to two pages long, preferably with fewer than 30 steps. At the top is a header that contains critical reference information: date of last revision, the objective written out in full, initials of authors, and the priority of the objective.

The body of the action plan is divided into several columns, as shown in Figure 16-1.

Using this comprehensive tool, you can write action plans that are clear to follow and easy to monitor and that ensure you attain your objective—but only if you take care as you write each step. The value of being this explicit in your action plans is that it makes it easier to merge strategic activity into your daily routine.

Choose Your Words Carefully

Communication is a key aspect of the action step. In effect, you are talking to yourself and other members of the planning team several months in the future. Those are the people who will be reading the action plan. So, you need to be precise because sometime down the road you're going to sit down and read a step and need to do it. Do what? If the action step is vague or fuzzy in any way, it may not lead to the intended result and you'll be in a lot of trouble.

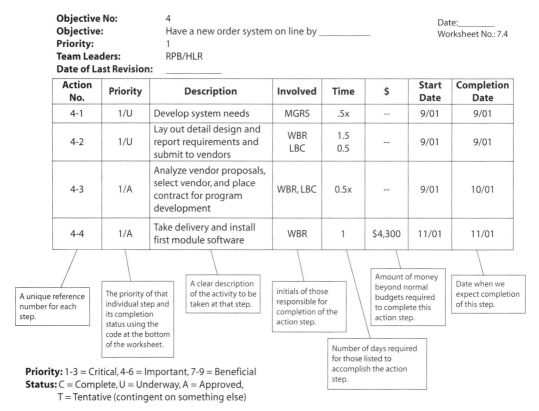

Objective No: 4
Objective: Have a new order system on line by _____
Priority: 1
Team Leaders: RPB/HLR
Date of Last Revision: _____

Date:_____
Worksheet No.: 7.4

Action No.	Priority	Description	Involved	Time	$	Start Date	Completion Date
4-1	1/U	Develop system needs	MGRS	.5x	--	9/01	9/01
4-2	1/U	Lay out detail design and report requirements and submit to vendors	WBR LBC	1.5 0.5	--	9/01	9/01
4-3	1/A	Analyze vendor proposals, select vendor, and place contract for program development	WBR, LBC	0.5x	--	9/01	10/01
4-4	1/A	Take delivery and install first module software	WBR	1	$4,300	11/01	11/01

A unique reference number for each step.

The priority of that individual step and its completion status using the code at the bottom of the worksheet.

A clear description of the activity to be taken at that step.

initials of those responsible for completion of the action step.

Number of days required for those listed to accomplish the action step.

Amount of money beyond normal budgets required to complete this action step.

Date when we expect completion of this step.

Priority: 1-3 = Critical, 4-6 = Important, 7-9 = Beneficial
Status: C = Complete, U = Underway, A = Approved,
     T = Tentative (contingent on something else)

Figure 16-1. The body of an action plan

Strategic Tip

Start each action step with a strong, clear action verb. Avoid vague words such as "consider" or "seek," because they don't really tell you what to do. But most of all, avoid "ponder." If the step says, "ponder world peace," you can think for a second and say, "OK, I've done that. I've pondered." Also avoid the verbs "plan" and "implement": they inevitably lead to a plan to plan, rather than to action.

You need to be specific about what you expect the end result of this step to be. In other words, instead of "Select software," you could say, "Identify three leading software packages, evaluate, and select one." Six months later, you'll know what to do.

Of course, if you don't use common sense, you can get too specific. You don't need an action plan that tells you to breathe or answer the telephone or pay your bills. If any step takes less than a half an hour, it probably can be encompassed into some other step in the action plan.

Make sure that each step is a true action step, not a milestone. Turn a passive milestone step like "contract review" into an active action step, "review and approve vendor contracts."

Finally, when you break down your objective into steps, don't craft steps that turn into ongoing activities. Rather than putting "improve quality at station #1," write an action step to establish a measurement system, assign responsibility, and set up a monitoring program.

Picking the People to Do the Work

Think about who would be the best person to do each step. Pick those who have the authority and responsibility to accomplish the task. When you list people on the action plan for specific action steps, you should note the *required* involvement of the senior managers, the people on the strategic planning team. But don't limit it to those people. Be sure to enlist others, remembering that you'll gain great time-efficiency by delegating activities to appropriate people outside the senior management team.

Be careful, however, not to get carried away listing people. Action plans can become very cumbersome if you try to list every person in the company who may be involved in a step. It's important to identify the senior manager and any other people who you suspect might have serious time constraints who must do some of the action steps: these are the people who will have the greatest difficulty allocating time and may require close management attention. Senior managers may delegate some of the details of action steps to those who work for them. If they do this, the senior managers must ensure that those to whom they delegate have the time and clear priority to be able to accomplish the task in the time bounded by the start and complete dates. Remember: it's the person listed who must make sure that the step gets done on time.

> **Strategic Tip**
>
> One reason to write an action plan before springing into action is to identify roadblocks before you start. Nothing will kill the enthusiasm for strategic planning faster than committing to a bunch of objectives and then not making any progress toward achievement. Consider a person's workload when assigning action steps.

Estimating the Time Required

How long is this step going to take?

For every action step, give a realistic estimate of the time it will take to complete. Round your estimates to the nearest half-day. Identify the amount of *dedicated time* (time spent working on this step and nothing else) necessary for the individuals listed to complete this step. Don't list elapsed time: this will be addressed with the start and complete dates. Use a dash to indicate less than a few hours or that the task will be delegated to people who work for the individual listed. If a step involves more than one person, list the time for each separately. If the time is the same for each of them, you can indicate the time for each person by using the "x" notation ("1x" indicates one day for each person listed). Do not list total "person-hours" for the step.

> **Strategic Tip**
>
> For most effective action plans, keep the time for each step to less than five days. If a step requires a top manager to spend more than five days doing that and nothing else, break it down into smaller chunks.

One of the most effective ways to get a realistic estimate of the time required for a step is simply to ask those who will be doing it to make the estimate. This approach not only gets realistic estimates, but also helps establish buy-in on the part of those who have to do the work. If you don't use this approach, you can expect considerable revisions to the time estimates as people review the action plans and realize that it commits them to getting this step done in the time indicated.

The Price of a Step

Some action steps will need more than time, maybe a few bucks as well. To keep things simple, don't list money for action items that are already covered in some existing budget. For example, if you have an established advertising budget that you will use to promote a new service, then you don't need to show any money on the action plan. But if your new service is in a totally different market so you have to take out new advertising in addition to your ongoing ad campaign, then you should show the incremental expenditure in the money column on the action plan.

When?

When will you start? When will you finish? These are important questions, but do not answer them until you are in the final planning meeting and can schedule them based on when you know what time and money you have available.

> **Strategic Tip**
>
> Don't budget money for the use of people's time if they're already on the payroll or in a hiring budget. However, for any new hires that are otherwise unplanned, show the cost (annual salary and benefits).

A Good Example

Figure 16-2 shows an example of a good, specific action plan (with start and complete dates left blank before the final meeting).

Thinking It Through

Now that you know the elements of an action plan, it's time to look at the process for writing one. Action plans will be written as assignments between the second and third meetings, so you need to give your team clear instructions so they do it right. The more work you do up front on writing the action plan, the easier it will be later on for you to execute the action plan.

The best approach is to start with an outline for the action plan. Do this right away so you can share it with others and get the planning team to buy into your approach before you spend too much time getting into the details. You can also use the outline to help you think about who should help you draft the plan. You should be sure to include people who will be involved in executing the action plan.

When the outline has been approved, the leader, the backup, and a few other people should figure out the details—the steps necessary, the people responsible for each step, and the cost and time involved. There's a lot to think about. As you draft the action plan, the details and sequence should start to become clear. If you have a logical sequence that leads you to reach the objective, then you have a good action plan.

So the next thing you should do is … nothing.

ACTION PLAN

Objective No: 3
Objective: Have a new computer on line by _____
Priority: 1
Team Leaders: RPB/HLR

Date: _____
Worksheet No.: 7.3

Action No.	Priority/ Status	Description	Involved	Time (Days)	$	Start Date	Completion Date
3-1	1/U	Review software needs	Mgrs	.5x	–		
3-2	1/U	Lay out detail design and distribution requirements	WBR LBC	1.5 0.5	–		
3-3	1/A	Analyze vendor proposals	WBR, LBC	–	–		
3-4	1/A	Take delivery of software	WBR	1	$4,300		
3-5	1/A	Design/write/debug distribution software	WBR, AHD	2x	$60,000		
3-6	3/A	Analyze outside software	WBR, LBC	3x	–		
3-7	5/A	Select personnel to evaluate software developed for operations	LBC	–	$100		
3-8	3/T	Select outside software	LBC, JWB	.5x	–		
3-9	1/A	Select hardware and peripherals	LBC, JWB	.5x	–		
3-10	1/A	Define finance options	LBC	.5	–		
3-11	1/A	Order hardware	LBC	–	?		
3-12	1/A	Order Datamax	LBC	–	–		
3-13	3/T	Order outside software	LBC	–	–		
3-14	1/A	Prepare site	AHD, RSA	2x	–		
3-15	3/A	Train Newark personnel (parallel)	AHD, WBR	3x	–		
3-16	1/A	Hardware delivery and installation	AHD	1	–		
3-17	1/T	Software delivery and installation	AHD, WBR	1x	$25,000		

Priority: 1-3 = Critical, 4-6 = Important, 7-9 = Beneficial
Status: C = Complete, U = Underway, A = Approved, T = Tentative (contingent on something else)

Figure 16-2. An example of an action plan

Time is a great filter of ideas. A little distance between fresh ideas and another look is just the thing to reveal holes in the first draft of the action plan.

Revise your work and distribute the second draft to the full planning team for review and feedback. They should look for missing steps, things out of sequence, and appropriate allocation of time and money. Take their feedback to heart and write a third draft before the final planning meeting.

> ### Strategic Tip
> If you don't go through at least three drafts of your action plan, it probably isn't ready. And writing three drafts the day before it's due won't cut it either. Time and reflection make for good action plans. The best approach is to draft your plan, let it sit for a week, and then draft it a second time. After that, bring it to the entire strategic planning team for their input and then put it through a final draft. If you follow these steps, you should be ready to achieve your objective.

Checklist for Good Action Plans

- ❏ Write an outline for the planning team to review.
- ❏ Form an action plan writing group of three to five people who will be involved in the execution of the plan.
- ❏ Expand the outline; brainstorm the steps and resources.
- ❏ Put the steps in sequence; write the first draft.
- ❏ Let the first draft sit for a week, then review and revise.
- ❏ Distribute the second draft for feedback from full planning team.
- ❏ Using feedback, write a third draft.

Before you can hold your final planning meeting to schedule these action plans, you need to know your capacity to do them. You need the budgets and time plans that we will develop in Chapter 17.

> ### Outside the Meeting
> Now that you know what makes for a good action plan and you have a process for writing one, go ahead and write an action plan using the format shown in Figure 16-2. Write one action plan for each of your objectives developed in Chapter 15 and listed in the Figure 15-4.

Plan Your Use of Resources: Money and Time

S O, CAN YOU PULL IT OFF? DO YOU KNOW WHAT IT TAKES? Do you have what it takes—time and money—to execute each specific part of your strategic plan?

Up to this point, presumably, you've done a good gut check of what you can and can't do and you haven't set yourself on any unreasonable course. Now it's time to add it all up to see if those presumptions are accurate. You need to make sure that you'll be able to do what you say you'll do. It's simple. If you don't have the time or the money to do what you say, you won't do it.

All along, you've been building a plan of what you're going to do and how you're going to do it. As you've gone through the process, people have made judgments about what is doable and what is not. Now it's time to test those judgments and lay it all out in an orderly, calculated manner.

Plan Your Use of Money

Money is a critical resource. Most managers understand budgeting, but how many organizations specifically link their strategic planning process to their budgeting? Specific planning leads to specific results, but it requires specific commitments of resources as well. In other words, if you want to accomplish something, you have to pay for it. Money, obviously, is a key part of the total strategic plan.

As we've emphasized for earlier steps in strategic planning, budgeting should not be complex. There are simple tools you can use to align your use of money with your strategic plan. Resource planning is essential: the better you plan, the greater your chance of reaching your objectives.

Start with Cash Flow

You need sustenance in a business. You can think of profits as the bread of business: you need some to remain strong, but you can go without it for a while if you have good reserves. Cash flow, however, is more like blood to your business. You will not survive without it even if you have great profits. So you must be careful, above all else, to guard your cash flow.

And, of course, it takes cash to do projects. It takes *extra* cash. So, how much cash do you have or can you get to fund your major projects?

> ### Strategic Tip
>
> Cash flow tends to get worse as a company grows. A growing company will need more working capital because accounts receivable and inventory (if there's inventory) will grow along with the company. There will likely be more money coming from rising sales, but it may not be received for 30 days or more. In the meantime, the company is paying for higher levels of operations (e.g., materials, labor, and other inputs), so it can become squeezed for cash without careful planning.

Project the Base Case

The idea of budgeting at this point in the process is to provide financial resources to fund your action plans. If, for any reason, the resources aren't there when you need them, your plans can come to a screeching halt. For this reason, you want good, conservative projections.

The operating budget and the cash flow budget are closely related, because profits are a key component of cash flow. However, the timing can be very different—especially in a growing business.

> ### Tales from the Strategy Vault
>
> Between the second and third sessions, ask your financial person to prepare a simple one-year operating budget (similar to Figure 17-1) and cash flow budget (similar to Figure 17-2) for inclusion in your plan.

Date:
Worksheet No.: 8.1

OPERATING BUDGET FOR 2001

	Jan	Feb	Mar	Apr	May	Jun	Jul	Aug	Sep	Oct	Nov	Dec	Total
Gross Sales	1,000,000	1,100,000	1,100,000	1,100,000	1,200,000	1,200,000	1,200,000	1,200,000	1,200,000	1,200,000	1,200,000	1,300,000	14,000,000
Deductions from Sales	64,000	71,000	71,000	71,000	77,000	77,000	77,000	77,000	77,000	77,000	77,000	84,000	900,000
Variations in Finished Goods & WIP	–	–	–	–	–	–	–	–	–	–	–	–	–
Net Sales After Inventory Adjustment	936,000	1,029,000	1,029,000	1,029,000	1,123,000	1,123,000	1,123,000	1,123,000	1,123,000	1,123,000	1,123,000	1,216,000	13,100,000
Materials	280,000	305,000	305,000	305,000	335,000	335,000	335,000	335,000	335,000	335,000	335,000	360,000	3,900,000
Labor	225,000	250,000	250,000	250,000	270,000	270,000	270,000	270,000	270,000	270,000	270,000	285,000	3,150,000
Payroll Taxes on Labor	20,000	23,000	23,000	23,000	25,000	25,000	25,000	25,000	25,000	25,000	25,000	26,000	290,000
Equipment Repairs	15,000	15,000	15,000	15,000	15,000	15,000	15,000	16,000	16,000	16,000	16,000	16,000	185,000
Manufacturing Expenses	19,000	21,000	21,000	21,000	24,000	24,000	24,000	24,000	24,000	24,000	24,000	25,000	275,000
Power & Light	9,000	9,000	9,000	9,000	11,000	11,000	11,000	11,000	11,000	11,000	11,000	12,000	125,000
Total Variable Costs	568,000	623,000	623,000	623,000	680,000	680,000	680,000	681,000	681,000	681,000	681,000	724,000	7,925,000
Gross Margin on Variable Costs	368,000	406,000	406,000	406,000	443,000	443,000	443,000	442,000	442,000	442,000	442,000	492,000	5,175,000
Supervision	10,000	10,000	10,000	10,000	10,000	10,000	10,000	10,000	10,000	10,000	10,000	10,000	120,000
Depreciation	40,000	40,000	40,000	40,000	40,000	40,000	40,000	40,000	45,000	45,000	45,000	45,000	500,000
Other Fixed Manufacturing Costs	60,000	60,000	55,000	50,000	50,000	50,000	50,000	50,000	50,000	55,000	60,000	60,000	650,000
Total Fixed Manufacturing Costs	110,000	110,000	105,000	100,000	100,000	100,000	100,000	100,000	105,000	110,000	115,000	115,000	1,270,000
Sales and Administrative Salaries	100,000	100,000	105,000	105,000	105,000	105,000	105,000	105,000	105,000	105,000	105,000	105,000	1,250,000
Advertising	5,000	5,000	15,000	5,000	5,000	15,000	5,000	5,000	15,000	5,000	5,000	15,000	100,000
Depreciation	5,000	5,000	5,000	5,000	5,000	5,000	5,000	5,000	5,000	5,000	5,000	5,000	60,000
Professional Services	15,000	5,000	5,000	35,000	5,000	5,000	5,000	5,000	5,000	5,000	5,000	5,000	100,000
Management Development	5,000	5,000	5,000	5,000	5,000	5,000	–	–	5,000	5,000	5,000	5,000	50,000
Pension	15,000	15,000	45,000	15,000	15,000	15,000	15,000	15,000	15,000	15,000	15,000	15,000	210,000
Other Sales & Administrative Costs	45,000	45,000	45,000	45,000	50,000	50,000	50,000	50,000	50,000	50,000	50,000	50,000	580,000
Total Sales and Administrative Costs	190,000	180,000	225,000	215,000	190,000	200,000	185,000	185,000	200,000	190,000	190,000	200,000	2,350,000
Interest Expense	25,000	25,000	25,000	25,000	25,000	25,000	25,000	25,000	25,000	25,000	25,000	25,000	300,000
Non-Operating Expenses	–	–	–	–	–	–	–	–	–	–	–	14,000	14,000
Net Income Before Taxes	43,000	91,000	51,000	66,000	128,000	118,000	133,000	132,000	112,000	117,000	112,000	138,000	1,241,000
Income Taxes	19,000	40,000	23,000	29,000	57,000	52,000	59,000	59,000	50,000	52,000	50,000	60,000	550,000
Net Income After Taxes	24,000	51,000	28,000	37,000	71,000	66,000	74,000	73,000	62,000	65,000	62,000	78,000	691,000

Figure 17-1. An example of an operating budget

Date: _____
Worksheet No.:8.3

CASH FLOW BUDGET FOR 2001

	Jan	Feb	Mar	Apr	May	Jun	Jul	Aug	Sep	Oct	Nov	Dec
Net Profit Before Taxes	43,000	91,000	51,000	66,000	128,000	118,000	133,000	132,000	112,000	117,000	112,000	138,000
+ Depreciation	45,000	45,000	45,000	45,000	45,000	45,000	45,000	45,000	50,000	50,000	50,000	50,000
- Taxes Paid				-78,000		-82,000						
- Scheduled Payments on Principal	-25,000	-25,000	-25,000	-25,000	-25,000	-25,000	-25,000	-25,000	-25,000	-25,000	-30,000	-30,000
- Increase in Accounts Receivable		-100,000			-100,000							-100,000
- Inc. in Inventories and Prepaid	-100,000			-100,000								-100,000
+ Inc. in Payables and Accrued Exp.	100,000			100,000								100,000
Cash Flow Generated	63,000	11,000	71,000	8,000	48,000	56,000	153,000	152,000	137,000	142,000	132,000	58,000
Investments	20,200	6,000	21,000	14,000	10,000	5,500	6,000	605,000	10,000	0	0	250,000
+ Unscheduled Payments on Principal									125,000	100,000		
+ Dividends												
Cash Consumed	20,200	6,000	21,000	14,000	10,000	5,500	6,000	605,000	135,000	100,000	0	250,000
Gross Cash Flow (Cash Flow Generated minus Cash Consumed)	42,800	5,000	50,000	-6,000	38,000	50,500	147,000	-453,000	2,000	42,000	132,000	-192,000
Liquidation of Unneeded Assets												
+ Funds Borrowed								125,000				
+ Equity Capital Obtained												
Cash Raised	0	0	0	0	0	0	0	125,000	0	0	0	0
Net Cash Flow (Gross Cash Flow plus Cash Raised)	42,800	5,000	50,000	-6,000	38,000	50,500	147,000	-328,000	2,000	42,000	132,000	-192,000
Cash Balance	99,916	104,916	154,916	148,916	186,916	237,416	384,416	56,416	58,416	100,416	232,416	40,416

Figure 17-2. An example of a cash flow budget

Timing of Investments

Strategic action plans cost money. You need to figure out how much, when, and whether you have it.

Ask your controller to go through the action plans between meetings, pull out all the action items that have money associated with them, and add up all those dollars. Compare that number, the total investment in action plans, with the cash resources available and see if you can do it. In other words, check to make sure that you'll have the cash available to meet action plan commitments over the coming year.

> ### Strategic Tip
>
> If your business is run well and you're doing strategic planning, there's a good chance someone will lend you money because most companies that think about the future are good risks. But you need enough cash flow to get the money you want to borrow. In other words, asking for $100,000 to meet payroll tomorrow is not a good way to earn your banker's confidence.

The key question in all this is cash flow. Will you have the cash in the bank to cover the normal costs of business and the expenses laid out in the action plan? If the answer is yes, you can go ahead and schedule the action plans with relatively few restraints.

If the answer is no, then you need a way to find the cash. There are a lot of ways to get money. You can sell assets, you can borrow, you can sell stock, or you can move more slowly on your action plans.

It's essential to remember that if you don't fund an action step, the action is unlikely to happen. Leaving critical action steps without funding will probably kill the entire action plan—and maybe even the objective. If you find you have financial constraints, you should use this budget to identify non-essential action steps that you may want to remove from the plan to free up resources for critical steps.

> ### Outside the Meeting
>
> Between the second and third sessions, ask your financial person to prepare a simple investment budget to include in your plan. This budget should be prioritized first according to the priority of each objective and second according to the priority of each action step, as shown in Figure 17-3.

INVESTMENT BUDGET

Date:_____
Worksheet No.: 8.2

Priority	Action Number	Item	Amount	Cumulative Amount	Outlay Date
1/1	3-4	Purchase software	4,300	4,300	
1/1	3-5	Develop software	60,000	64,300	
1/1	3-17	Purchase software	25,000	89,300	
2/1	1-2	Develop incentive bonus plan	3,000	92,300	
3/1	4-3	Purchase various materials	16,000	108,300	
3/7	8-14	Develop new mailing pieces	21,000	129,300	
4	–	Bobst die cutter	600,000	729,300	
5/1	6-6	Design cost system	10,000	739,300	
6/1	9-5	Acquisition search	12,000	751,300	
6/1	9-24	Acquisition negotiations	5,500	756,800	
6/1	9-29	Acquisition close	250,000?	1,006,800	
7/1	10-4	Conduct field survey	5,000	1,011,800	

Figure 17-3. A simple investment budget

Prioritize Action Plans

You may not be able to do everything, but you should do as many of the action plans as you can completely fund. There will be certain action plans that you can take more than a year to do. You may wish to partially fund such action plans, understanding that you can finish them next year. After all, there's no reason why all action plans must be completed within 12 months. If you put together an action plan that says an objective will take 14 months to complete, that's OK.

But if you cannot fund a plan through to completion or at least to a reasonable point of completion, it may be best to put it aside and review it next year when you do strategic planning again.

A Story of AOL's Shaky Road to Growth

In 1997 America Online greatly increased its subscriber base. With a complete change in its pricing policy, the company went from about 5 or 6 million subscribers to 14 million in a matter of months. That sudden growth caused huge bottlenecks in the dial-in networks. It seemed that every AOL subscriber, new or old, was angry with the company.

Sure, prices were for the most part lower because AOL had dramatically changed its policy from an hourly charge to a monthly flat fee. But, now the network was so crowded that customers often couldn't connect. There were more than twice as many subscribers with the same number of dial-in connections to serve them. And because AOL had changed to a flat rate, those who were able to connect were staying online a *long* time.

AOL was like the dog that caught the car: its marketing was too successful and it couldn't handle all of the resulting business. The company was stretched for resources and facing a dilemma. The managers didn't want to back off on rapidly growing the customer base, but they did not have the resources to grow the physical network quickly enough to keep pace. AOL was at risk of losing customers as fast as they signed up.

The managers needed to do something—and quick. They examined their options and prioritized. They realized that, as the Internet evolved, the value of their service was moving from dial-up networks to content. So they sold the physical network portion of their business to MCI-WorldCom. They used the cash from that transaction, along with other borrowed money, to fund their core business, which was taking care of their subscribers and generating content. They advertised like crazy and continually improved their content.

The plan worked. MCI-WorldCom used its strategic competencies to do what it does best—build a world-class computer network for AOL—and AOL was able to generate the resources to keep most of its customers and continue growing. Now AOL is the No. 1 choice for Internet access: about 60% of all new Internet users choose to enter with AOL.

Five-Year Operating Statement

Look forward five years.

What will be the results of your strategic planning five years from now? Will it work? How well will it work?

What are your results of your strategy going to be? How will your revenues grow? How about your costs? In the five-year operating statement, you roll all of the good stuff together to get a sense of the financial impact of your strategic vision. You roll in the growth of your markets, all your market share gain, any markets you're exiting, any new products you're launching, opportunities you're pursuing, and threats that may hurt you.

> **Tales from the Strategy Vault**
>
> One company we worked with was very gung-ho about going after commodity markets in the first stages of strategic planning. But then they did a five-year operating budget and realized that, if they pursued their chosen strategy, their profits would be significantly lower in five years. So they did a very strategic thing: they said "no" to that option. Strategy, after all, is often more about what you say "no" to than what you decide to pursue.

The purpose of this exercise is to enable you to see how you think your plans will work. This is where you add it all up and check to see if your math and logic match up to create a more profitable company. The idea here is to do a sanity check on your strategy, to catch things ahead of time.

Another advantage of the five-year operating statement is that it may help uncover problems that will arise from success. For instance, if you think the company will grow 50% a year, the five-year projection might help you realize you'll need to hire more people and maybe even acquire or build a new facility. At the very least, it can serve as a warning to your employees that their jobs are about to change quite a bit in the next five years.

Be sure to build new costs into your budget. Some costs are subtle, rising with the complexity associated with a larger business. You can easily miss some overhead costs, for example, if you don't look and look again.

> **Tales from the Strategy Vault**
>
> In six years, General Fasteners grew nearly tenfold and much of the growth involved adding branches. The managers started to notice that new branches had problems getting up and running because there were problems of staffing, systems installations, and inventory management that had to be resolved every time a new branch went live. As a result, each branch took a long time to become profitable. Looking five years down the road, it was easy to see that continued rapid growth would only make matters worse, ultimately leading to a severe cash flow problem. So, the company laid out a new system for opening branches quickly and easily. This process turned a potential disaster into a significant source of strategic strength.

Budget Your Time—It's the Smartest Kind of Budgeting

Strategy is important, exciting stuff. So why don't we just implement it all tomorrow? It sure would be nice.

The reason, of course, is that people run out of time. This problem is so universal, and so central to strategic success, that we're amazed at how little attention people have paid to it. Yet it's painfully true that, for most companies, one of the most critical elements of strategic success is where the members of the top management team spend their time.

> **Outside the Meeting**
>
> Between the second and third sessions, ask your financial person to prepare a simple five-year operating statement, similar to that shown in Figure 17-4, for inclusion in your plan. This pro forma should include as many financial aspects your strategy as feasible—revenue projections, direct cost projections, overhead projections, market growth, opportunities, threats, etc.

One of the most common problems that we must all deal with is that eventually we run out of the most precious resource—the productive time of smart people. Managers, after all, are very busy. Unfortunately, while every well-managed company in the world budgets money, very few budget time. And it's much more important to budget time because, unlike money, there's only so much of it. You can't go to the bank and get more.

Time must be allocated efficiently by priority, because there's not enough time to do everything and some things are more important than others. Time management is always a tough discipline, but in strategic planning it becomes critical. Strategic planning helps you figure out who is going to do what, and when.

Remember that time isn't free. Once you've used time, you can't get it back. If, for instance, you need your vice president of marketing to do something and he doesn't have enough time to do it, you can't exactly get another vice president of marketing in two minutes.

The key in time management is to make sure your most important people are spending their time on the most important projects. Using the time management process links a manager's available time to the key projects in the company.

FIVE-YEAR OPERATING STATEMENT

Date: _____
Worksheet No.: 8.4

	$2000	%2000	$2001	%2001	$2002	%2002	$2003	%2003	$2004	%2004	$2005	%2005
Gross Sales	14,000,000	106.9	16,000,000	107.4	19,000,000	107.3	22,000,000	107.3	26,000,000	107.4	30,000,000	107.5
Deductions from Sales	900,000	6.9	1,100,000	7.4	1,300,000	7.3	1,500,000	7.3	1,800,000	7.4	2,100,000	7.5
Variations in Finished Goods & WIP	—		—		—		—		—		—	
Net Sales After Inventory Adjustment	13,100,000	100.0	14,900,000	100.0	17,700,000	100.0	20,500,000	100.0	24,200,000	100.0	27,900,000	100.0
Materials	3,900,000	29.8	4,400,000	29.5	5,200,000	29.4	6,000,000	29.3	7,100,000	29.3	8,150,000	29.2
Labor	3,150,000	24.0	3,500,000	23.5	4,100,000	23.2	4,700,000	22.9	5,500,000	22.7	6,300,000	22.6
Payroll Taxes on Labor	290,000	2.2	325,000	2.1	380,000	2.1	440,000	2.1	515,000	2.1	590,000	2.1
Equipment Repairs	185,000	1.4	225,000	1.5	265,000	1.5	320,000	1.6	385,000	1.6	445,000	1.6
Manufacturing Expenses	275,000	2.1	330,000	2.2	405,000	2.3	495,000	2.4	580,000	2.4	670,000	2.4
Power & Light	125,000	1.0	180,000	1.2	265,000	1.5	370,000	1.8	510,000	2.1	670,000	2.4
Total Variable Costs	7,925,000	60.5	8,960,000	60.1	10,615,000	60.0	12,325,000	60.1	14,590,000	60.3	16,825,000	60.3
Gross Margin on Variable Costs	5,175,000	39.5	5,940,000	39.9	7,085,000	40.0	8,175,000	39.9	9,610,000	39.7	11,075,000	39.7
Supervision	120,000	0.9	135,000	0.9	155,000	0.9	180,000	0.9	210,000	0.9	250,000	0.9
Depreciation	500,000	3.8	550,000	3.7	650,000	3.7	750,000	3.7	900,000	3.7	1,050,000	3.8
Other Fixed Manufacturing Costs	650,000	5.0	750,000	5.0	900,000	5.1	1,060,000	5.2	1,230,000	5.1	1,400,000	5.0
Total Fixed Manufacturing Costs	1,270,000	9.7	1,435,000	9.6	1,705,000	9.6	1,990,000	9.7	2,340,000	9.7	2,700,000	9.7
Sales and Administrative Salaries	1,250,000	9.5	1,375,000	9.2	1,600,000	9.0	1,800,000	8.8	2,000,000	8.3	2,300,000	8.2
Advertising	100,000	0.8	135,000	0.9	175,000	1.0	225,000	1.1	300,000	1.2	335,000	1.2
Depreciation	60,000	0.5	70,000	0.5	90,000	0.5	115,000	0.6	145,000	0.6	155,000	0.6
Professional Services	100,000	0.8	110,000	0.7	120,000	0.7	135,000	0.7	170,000	0.7	195,000	0.7
Management Development	50,000	0.4	55,000	0.4	60,000	0.3	65,000	0.3	75,000	0.3	85,000	0.3
Pension	210,000	1.6	280,000	1.9	330,000	1.9	385,000	1.9	455,000	1.9	525,000	1.9
Other Sales & Administrative Costs	580,000	4.4	650,000	4.4	750,000	4.2	860,000	4.2	1,000,000	4.1	1,150,000	4.1
Total Sales and Administrative Costs	2,350,000	17.9	2,675,000	18.0	3,125,000	17.7	3,585,000	17.5	4,145,000	17.1	4,745,000	17.0
Interest Expense	300,000	2.3	375,000	2.5	350,000	1.8	250,000	1.1	90,000	0.3	—	0.0
Non-Operating Expenses	14,000	0.1	14,000	0.1	15,000	0.1	20,000	0.1	20,000	0.1	25,000	0.1
Net Income Before Taxes	1,241,000	9.5	1,441,000	9.7	1,890,000	9.9	2,330,000	10.6	3,015,000	11.6	3,605,000	12.0
Income Taxes	550,000	4.2	652,000	4.4	859,000	4.5	1,061,000	4.8	1,376,000	5.3	1,648,000	5.5
Net Income After Taxes	691,000	5.3	789,000	5.3	1,031,000	5.4	1,269,000	5.8	1,639,000	6.3	1,957,000	7.5

Figure 17-4. An example of a five-year operating statement

You'll force people to figure out the most efficient use of their time and you'll help them use it better. Time budgeting gets people organized and focused on the right things.

The CEO of a Hotdog Stand

Think about the CEO of a hotdog stand and how he budgets his time. He has both strategic and nonstrategic responsibilities.

His job is filled with routine, nonstrategic things, such as making hot dogs, selling hot dogs, buying more hot dogs to make and sell, and buying mustard and ketchup and soda too. He has many routine responsibilities. He does not have a lot of time to do strategic planning, because every day that he spends on strategic planning he's not selling any hot dogs.

On the other hand, the CEO of a large multinational hotdog corporation can spend three months on strategic planning if he or she wants, because someone else is actually making the hotdogs.

Two Types of Activity

The point here is to understand how much time must be spent on routine things and how much is available for special projects. Most managers should have some of each. The more strategically oriented your job is, the more time you should reserve for nonroutine activities. Conversely, those with job functions that are critical to day-to-day operations will find they have less time available for special projects. It's possible to do both, however, and that's why small-company managers can feel very stressed. To get a better handle on time, let's define the two types of activity we want to examine—routine time and special projects.

Routine Time

People have jobs: they've got to do stuff. Every day, stuff's got to get done. Day after day after day, people have to take care of the routine if your company is going to continue to operate. And your key management people probably have to do a lot of that stuff.

There are basic requirements for the company. The CFO has to do monthly projections of financial statements. The marketing director must do brochures and meet with advertising agencies. The operations person must keep the plant running. Everyone has some routine work that must be done every single month.

Sometimes the Unexpected Is Routine

In most managerial jobs, a certain amount of time each month will be devoted to unexpected problems. This should be built into the calculation of routine time—maybe a day or so a month for most managers, but possibly much more for, say, a manufacturing plant manager. But you should not build in a buffer to allow for huge disasters. That's why you leave open nights and weekends. Save those for the disasters.

We really mean this. If you routinely work nights and weekends, you may not have any buffer—which could make the effect of disasters on your business much worse. (In addition, you're probably headed for burnout.) So reserve that time for "re-creation" and emergencies.

Sometimes the Routine Is Focused Wrong

When companies begin to examine how their people spend their routine time, they can find the focus is wrong. For example, it's not uncommon to find that a company with a stated focus on small customers spends a significant amount of chasing big companies. It strokes the ego of the salesperson and, probably, other managers in the company. But they could make a lot more money by dealing with smaller "Ma and Pa type" customers—who offer higher margins. Finding out specifically how people spend their time is very valuable.

Chart It Out: Time Worksheet

The best way to figure out how much routine time you have is to put it down on paper. Spend a few minutes at the end of a day to list your major activities and how much time you spent on each. If you do this for two weeks, you'll have a good idea how you spend time. Then you can easily organize it into five categories—daily, weekly, monthly, quarterly, or annual activities—and fill out the time worksheet shown in Figure 17-5.

Outside the Meeting

Between the second and third sessions, ask each team member to develop a time worksheet (Figure 17-5) and a personal annual schedule (Figure 17-6). (An easy-to-use electronic spreadsheet template for both of these forms can be downloaded free from our Web site, www.simplifiedstrategy.com.)

Using a completed time worksheet, you can then show your routine time commitments over the next 12 months using the personal annual schedule (Figure 17-6). Fill in the number of workdays per month in the Gross Days Available row. Then, subtract your annual, quarterly, monthly, weekly, and daily tasks that

Date:_____
TIME WORKSHEET FOR: *BKS (plant manager)*   Worksheet No.: 9.1

Regular Time Plan Functional Activity	Daily Activity	Weekly Activity	Monthly Activity	Quarterly Activity	Annual Activity
AM Staff Meeting	.5 hr				
Plant Tour	1.0 hr				
Interruptions and Problems	2.0 hr				
Department Meetings		1.0 hr			
Management Meetings		1.0 hr	1 day		
Weekly Planning		2.0 hr			
Performance Reviews			1.0 hr		
Wage Reviews				1 day, FMAN	
Bonus Communications				.5 day JAJO	
Education				2 days MJSD	
Coaching		1.0 hr			
Evaluations				2 days JAJO	
Board Meetings				2 days FMAN	
Strategic Planning					4 days JFA
Vacation					15 days Jun
Total Days	.4 days	.5 days	1.1 days	7.5 days	19 days

Figure 17-5. An example of a time worksheet

Time Required for Action Plans in Priority Sequence

Action Plan # 3	Priority 1	4 days	Action Plan # 10	Priority 7	0 days
Action Plan # 5	Priority 1	7 days	Action Plan # Bobst	Priority 4	15 days
Action Plan # 1	Priority 2	25 days	Action Plan #	Priority	days
Action Plan # 4	Priority 3	1.5 days	Action Plan #	Priority	days
Action Plan # 9	Priority 3	4 days	Action Plan #	Priority	days
Action Plan # 8	Priority 3	0 days	Action Plan #	Priority	days
Action Plan # 6	Priority 5	3 days	Action Plan #	Priority	days
Action Plan # 7	Priority 5	9 days	Action Plan #	Priority	days
Action Plan # 2	Priority 7	5 days	Action Plan #	Priority	days
				Total	**73.5 days**

Figure 17-5. (continued)

PERSONAL ANNUAL SCHEDULE FOR: *BKS (Plant Manager)*

Date: _____
Worksheet No.: 9.2-1

		May	June	July	August
Gross Days Available		22	21	21	23
Regular Annual Days		–	15	–	–
Regular Quarterly Days		3	2	2.5	3
Regular Monthly Days		1.1	1.1	1.1	1.1
Regular Weekly Days		2	.5	2	2
Regular Daily Days		8.8	2.4	8.4	9.2
Net Days Available		**7.1**	**0**	**7.0**	**7.7**
Description	**Action Number**	**May**	**June**	**July**	**August**
Teach system to supervisors	3-2	2.5			
Monitor rejects	5-1	.5	.5	.5	.5
Participative mgt. training	1-10	2.5		2	
Develop incentive program	1-13			4.5	4
Develop fix-up details	4-4				1
Review material program	7-3				2
Review market study	2-6	1.5			
Total		**7**	**.5**	**7**	**7.5**

Figure 17-6. An example of personal annual schedule, showing one-third of a calendar year

fall in each month from the gross days. That leaves the Net Days Available, the number of days you have for special projects in the month listed.

> **Strategic Tip**
>
> Be sure to include such things as trade shows, next year's strategic planning, and especially vacation time. This process is very efficient at filling every available moment of time. If you do not plan for your vacation, you'll fill that time with other commitments and find you have no time left for vacation.

Honesty is a key requirement of a time worksheet. People need to refrain from putting things on the routine list that are not necessary. For instance, it would be nice for a manager to read five journals a month, but it probably isn't necessary and shouldn't be marked as routine time.

No one, of course, believes they waste time. This tool helps people understand how they're actually spending their time.

Often people think it's a badge of honor to have a large amount of routine time. But we would argue that it's the weakest managers who have the most routine time, because they're unable to delegate the work. Another

> **Strategic Tip**
>
> Our experience shows that the first year a typical top manager goes through this time planning process it's common to have about 10% percent of the time (about 25 days a year) available for special projects. If you have less than this, you should scrutinize your work for errors and consider how you can reduce your routine commitments.

problem weak managers may have is trying to do everything because they're unable to prioritize.

Those who have used this simple time planning tool in conjunction with simplified strategic planning report significant changes in their behavior over a few years. Initially, managers notice for the first time exactly how they spend their time. Their reaction is often, "No wonder

I don't have time to get other things done." The second thing that often happens is managers begin to empower the people below them to do the more routine stuff, so that they can focus more on the strategic things that will drive the company forward. Both reactions have profound impact on the productivity of a company.

Keep Doing What You've Always Done and You'll Keep Getting What You've Always Gotten

You want to do more than the routine. After all, the idea of simplified strategic planning is to move forward. We have found that companies need to reduce the routine time in a manager's schedule to no more than 60% to 80%, depending on the size of the company. They need to devote a good portion of their time to special projects that move the company forward.

Using the time worksheet and the personal annual schedule, each manager can determine how much of his or her time is consumed by routine activities and how much is available for special projects.

Determine the Time Required by Action Plans

Go to each action plan one at a time. Look at each step and ask the manager in charge of each step to make a time commitment to do that step. Add up each person's time required for each action plan.

Then add up the amount committed by each person to all action plans.

Finally, compare each person's time required for all action plans with his or her time available over the next 12 months.

Some people will have plenty of time available, some will just squeak through, and many (especially on the first run through this exercise) will have little or no time free from routine activities.

Options for Those Who Need More Time

Action plans must get done or else you will not be driving the company forward. Good managers must find a way to alter their schedule or work pattern so that they can have time to do the strategic things to make your company better.

There are four options:

- **Delegation**: Find other people in the company to do the routine so that you can do the strategic projects. Or delegate the strategic project work.
- **Reduction**: Reduce the amount of time you spend on routine things or on action plans. It's often possible to do a little less and still be fine.
- **Elimination**: Get rid of some routine things that aren't necessary. And in an action plan, some steps may not be necessary. It never hurts to look again.
- **Postponement**: Postpone an action plan. You've got to keep up with routine activities, but action plans—unfortunately—can be postponed.

Schedule

Now that you've done your best to balance time and money availability and requirements, it's time to schedule action plans. But first, you'll need to prioritize them so that you know which ones are the most important. Then, you'll apply resources to the higher-priority plans first.

> **Tales from the Strategy Vault**
>
> We once met a highly paid executive who kept a ball of string in his office. Whenever anyone in the office received a package, he cut off the string and saved it on the ball. A child of the depression, he was being frugal. But he could have put his time to much better use.

After you prioritize the action plans, you'll need to figure out which ones you can afford and which ones you have time to do. When you commit to getting something done during a certain month, you actually have to do it then.

Individuals keep score on their personal annual schedules. Each person records how much time is committed in any given month to the routine and how much is allocated to the specific action steps. When you run out of available time in a given month, you have to stop scheduling things and push them out to a later date. A personal annual schedule forces a manager to schedule activities month to month, spread out over the year.

It's taken a few hours, but you should now have a complete set of action plans with all required resources identified and a schedule that individuals have created based on the time *they feel* they have available. It's critical to follow all of these steps as prescribed, because this is the process that brings real commitment, not just lip service, to achieving the objectives.

This final meeting results in commitments. We want to eliminate the excuses of "I ran out of time" or "I ran out of money." It *is* a tough discipline, but it can be taught and it is crucial. People who use this information will find it *very* effective in helping them get things done. And when individuals get things done, you're more likely to achieve your strategic objectives.

In the Meeting

In the third meeting, review and schedule action plans in the following sequence:

1. Review and approve action plans and resources required.
2. Review time available versus time required for each person. After making any necessary adjustments, determine if there are any constraints that would force postponement of some action plans.
3. Review financial budgets to determine if there are any constraints.
4. Schedule action plans in priority order, with individuals making commitments that are recorded on their personal annual schedules and action plan leaders recording commitments with start and complete dates for each action plan.

chapter 18

Use the Plan

A PLAN IS USELESS IF NOT USED FREQUENTLY. Furthermore, to be of real value, it must be used for more than impressing friends and squashing large bugs. Such a plan, though quite good for the ego and pest control, isn't going to help your bottom line.

A plan is useless if no one looks at it. A good plan is a living document that becomes part of the culture of the company. It's not enough just to have a plan. The idea of business is to get something done. So do it. Use the plan. Get people to live it, breathe it, and eat it.

It sounds like an obvious step, but it is frequently overlooked. The plan may make it obvious who does what when, and yet the plan needs buy-in—and not just from the folks who created it. You need to spread the word to everyone affected. You also have to check in along the way and monitor what you're doing. And *every year* you need to go through the entire process to see how circumstances (and your assumptions) have changed.

The plan is a tool. If you've done a good, creative job of thinking about the future, and if your analysis of the information has produced a set of cohesive action plans, you'll want to make sure your work doesn't go to waste. To do this, you need to be sure that using the plan becomes a routine part of working at your company. It should not be something outside what people do in their jobs. The challenge is to make strategic thinking and strategic action part of the routine.

Strategic planning is also a recursive process that produces better results when the planners learn from planning. Time and experience are great teachers. The more years you put into strategic planning, the better you get at it and the easier the process becomes. When people approach this process with a memory of previous years of planning, they remember what came up in the past and what worked. They learn. The companies that stick with this process and treat it as part of their normal course of business are the ones that benefit most. They learn to state what they want to accomplish, and then they accomplish it.

Spread the Word

To get anything done in your company, you need more than your top people involved. You need to spread the word about your strategy so that everyone in the company understands what you're trying to do. The most important word to spread is your vision—the sense of where you're going. You need buy-in.

It's not necessary to make a grand or complicated announcement. More important than any announcement is the overall new tone of the company. While you may kick things off with a formal announcement, communicating the plan means making it truly a part of the company. You communicate the plan by your actions. You communicate it every day with everything you do and every word you print or say. But the real communication is your actual behavior.

Develop a simple communication plan so that you have a systematic approach to spreading the word. You can mention the vision in the company newsletter or have the

> **Tales from the Strategy Vault**
>
> Long before the public ever heard the slogan "Quality is Job 1" from Ford, the message had been hammered home internally. Everyone in the company and even those outside such as suppliers were forced to live, breathe, and accept Q1 as a basic philosophy. Only when Ford was sure it was living up to its vision for quality did "Quality is Job 1" show up in the advertising.

president give a five-minute speech explaining what has been done, where the company expects to be, and when it expects to be there. And then it must become part of the culture. People will scrutinize all actions that aren't true to the vision, but they will understand and appreciate the actions that are. And action is communication. So, your communication—all of it—must be consistent with your vision. If it is, you will win.

Monthly Check-In

If you hit the accelerator on your car, close your eyes, and drive for three minutes on a busy highway, you're likely to end up in a horrible disaster. Similarly, if you write your strategy and then put your head down for three years hoping you will follow it, you're liable to find yourself in a disaster.

> ### In the Meeting
> Develop a brief communication plan. Identify the audiences to whom you want to communicate some elements of the strategic plan. For each audience describe in a few words:
> - the message
> - the media or forum for communication
> - the person responsible for delivering the message
> - the schedule for completing the communication
>
> This should take about 15 minutes at the end of the final meeting.

Instead, we recommend that you check in once in a while and center yourself and your company with regard to your strategy. Make sure the strategy is still moving down the highway in the right direction and not running off to the side.

It should be a brief check-in, an hour meeting once a month. Every action plan has actionable items. Are they getting done? For the most part, you should be able to review all on-target action plans in a half an hour. The second half-hour should be used to deal with problems. How are you going to get those plans back on track?

Just because you wrote something on paper doesn't guarantee that it's going to happen. You have to keep an eye on all the action plans because strategic planning doesn't work on auto-pilot. The team members must be constantly checking in and trying to hold themselves accountable for what they said they were going to get done. Otherwise, the tendency will be to drift off target.

> ### Strategic Tip
> If these meetings begin to take more than an hour, that's a good indicator that something is very wrong with your process. There's something wrong either with the commitment or with the way you run the meeting. Figure out the cause of the problem and get things on track. Otherwise, you risk killing enthusiasm for the strategy process.

Certainly, in these meetings, discussion often stimulates other discussion. There may be discussion about difficulties executing a particular element of your strategy or vision. There's a range of topics you can discuss, but you have to remember that this meeting is scheduled to review what's happening. You must actively manage your strategy.

Quarterly Tune-Up

Four times a year you want to pull out your assumptions and see if they still make sense. Do they still portray the way you expect the world to be? Do you still believe them? If the outside world changes enough to invalidate your assumptions, you probably need to step back, reexamine your strategies and possibly your objectives, and see if they are still in line with reality.

Slight changes in assumptions probably won't warrant much change in your strategic planning. For instance, for most companies, if the assumption of growth changed from 4.5% to 4.6%, it probably wouldn't make a significant difference in their strategy. But a big change—from 4.5% to 14%—would likely necessitate a change in course.

Mostly, this meeting will be one in which you reaffirm your assumptions and make sure nothing radical has come up. If anything arises, it's most commonly the need to watch an assumption more closely—and that's good to know.

Planning the Plan: Going Full Circle

Strategic planning is an ongoing process, not a one-time event. It's easy to think that once you do strategic planning you're done. That works, of course, in only one impossible situation—if there's no change in your world. But the real world changes over time, and so must your plan.

A plan is great as long as it's a living document—and *not* a straitjacket that prevents appropriate reactions to change.

So update the plan *once a year*. Go through the entire process all over again. With the experience you'll have gained, it shouldn't take quite as long. For most companies, four days of meeting time (a one-day first session, two days for the second session, and a one-day final session) should be sufficient to update the vision for changes in the environment.

Tales from the Strategy Vault

The old Soviet Union's form of government was an example of how a five-year plan, written in stone, does not work. Everything was locked in, except for a small thing that no one in the whole Communist world could possibly envision—change.

Remember: these are not one-year plans we're talking about, but rather plans with three- to five-year time horizons. You probably don't have to change a lot. The point is to tune things up enough so that you feel confident to run at full speed for a good year. So go through it all again.

You'll learn as you go, of course. The second year you'll ask what worked and what didn't and you should begin to see patterns. The core of all good business is learning, and this is a great learning process. We've seen many companies go through this process; it's very interesting to see the differences between their first-year plan and one they put together after five years. Even though the first-year plan was good, it still looked like a crayon painting next to a Rembrandt when compared with their fifth-year plan. This process is about continuous learning.

Remember that every year you need to

- Review
- Revise
- Reassess and
- Resolve to do what's necessary to adjust to changes.

Every year, it gets easier. Figure 18-1 provides a specific look at the monitoring process and how long it should take.

In the Meeting

Before leaving the final meeting, establish a monitoring schedule as shown in Figure 18-2. This should include specific dates and times for each monthly meeting, each quarterly meeting, and next year's annual update. There should be no acceptable excuse for missing these meetings.

Course Corrections

The heart of your strategic plan will usually remain more or less the same. Your vision, strategy, mission, and goals will most likely change little from year to year. However, from year to year the objectives and implementation will usually change a great deal. The vision remains constant while your way of getting there may have to adjust to changing conditions. You complete your objectives and move on to new ones. Or, some of your

MONITORING PROCESS

MONTHLY	
Action Plan Leaders/Backups	15-30 min.
▪ Drive the plan; keep actions, people, and dates on track	
Action Plan Teams	15-60 min.
▪ Resolve any shorfall in action plans	
▪ Modify AP as needed, based on new information	
▪ Plan specific dates for meetings next month	
Strategic Planning Team	30-60 min.
▪ Review AP for completion of steps	
QUARTERLY	
Strategic Planning Team	2-6 hrs.
▪ Review assumptions (section 4)	
▪ Review and revise strategy (section 5)	
▪ Review and revise objectives and resulting APs (sections 6 and 7)	
▪ Reschedule all APs to get on track	
ANNUALLY	
Strategic Planning Team	4 days
▪ Reassess and update entire strategic plan, review and revise all sections as needed	
▪ Revise plan for new developments in the environment	
▪ Set new objectives to drive strategy implementation over next 12 to 18 months	

Figure 18-1. How the monitoring process works

objectives may be pushed back a year by tougher conditions than you'd assumed. But usually, you won't be making many course corrections.

Simplified Strategic Planning

This process is about logic. You analyze your present situation and your vision of the future. Then, you figure a way to win in that future, while constantly modifying the plan based on real-life changes. Winning is about doing what you really want to do. So, what do you really want to do? Write it down and follow the plan. And enjoy the victory.

MONITORING SCHEDULE

Date: _____
Worksheet No.: 9.4

Monitoring Meeting Coordinator	BKS
Monitoring Meeting Leader	GFM
Standard Monitoring Meeting	Second Friday of every month, 10:00 am, conference room
Special Arrangements	If you need to join the meeting by telephone, you must make arrangements through BKS no later than one business day before the meeting. NO EXCUSES!
Handouts	Any handouts you want to circulate need to be given to BKS no less than two business days before the meeting (email submissions are OK).

Current Meeting Schedule

Date	Time	Location	Agenda
Friday, 10/10	10:00 am-11:00 am	Conference room	Monthly meeting
Friday, 11/14	10:00 am-11:00 am	Conference room	Monthly meeting
Friday, 12/12	8:00 am-12 noon	Conference room	Quarterly meeting
Friday, 1/9	8:00 am-9:00 am	Conference room	Monthly meeting
Friday, 2/13	10:00 am-11:00 am	Conference room	Monthly meeting
Monday, 3/16	1:00 pm-5:00 pm	Hilton, Buffalo Grove, IL (before the sales meeting)	Quarterly meeting
Thursday, 4/9	10:00 am-11:00 am	Conference room	Monthly meeting
Friday, 5/8	10:00 am-11:00 am	Conference room	Monthly meeting
Friday, 6/12	8:00 am-5:00 pm	Johnson Conference Center	Annual meeting 1
Monday, 7/6	10:00 am-11:00 am	Conference room	Monthly meeting
Thursday, 7/30 & Friday 7/31	8:00 am-5:00 pm (both days)	Hyatt, Lake Tahoe	Annual meeting 2
Friday, 8/21	10:00 am-11:00 am	Conference call	Monthly meeting
Friday, 9/11	8:00 am-5:00 pm	Johnson Conference Center	Annual meeting 3

Figure 18-2. An example of a monitoring schedule

This is a real chance for you to control your destiny. You can move your company forward with vision and logic if you follow this simplified process. It's doable and easy. Follow the steps. Do it again and again, year to year, and you will see that this is no flavor of the month. This is the real deal—simplified strategic planning is how to win.

Epilogue

WHAT WE HAVE GIVEN YOU IN THIS BOOK—*Simplified Strategic Planning*—is a usable tool. You can do this in your own company. Use the schedule in Chapter 3. Fill out the worksheets.

If your company is like most of the companies we've worked with, you'll be astonished with the results you get. We've seen an average of 12% sales growth and 23% profit growth *per year* in companies that we work with using this process over long periods of time. In the first year of using this process, most companies have achieved more than 24% in sales growth and a 49% increase in profits.

To this end, we want to help you get started by providing some of the forms you'll need to fill out in using this process. To obtain these forms, use a Web browser to access www.simplifiedstrategy.com and select "Resources from the book." You may also e-mail us any questions you may have about simplified strategic planning.

These tools will be a great help in getting started—and remember: failure to start is the single deadliest problem in the planning process. But if you get started and then follow through with the planning process, you will:

- Take control of your destiny
- Gain a better understanding of your business environment
- Improve the assumptions you make about your company's future
- Make more appropriate strategic choices that will sharpen your focus
- Turn this vision into meaningful involvement for your management team
- Get results by monitoring your progress and adapting your plan to changes in the real world.

Well, there you have it. You start with ideas, information, and assumptions. Synthesize them into strategies and supporting objectives. Give your plan some teeth with action plans, budgets, and schedules.

If you follow the process laid out in this book, you'll get results. More important, you'll be consciously choosing the direction in which your company is moving and you'll be actively pushing the company in the direction you choose.

We cannot overemphasize the points made in the beginning of this book: strategic management is not separate from your normal work—it should be part of it. The most successful companies we have worked with have all said the same thing: one of the greatest benefits of strategic planning is that it helps the management team to think strategically in the course of day-to-day business. That's real strategic management. These companies have done more than make a plan; they've lived the plan.

Appendix

The following table gives you the list of worksheets in this book that are used in *Simplified Strategic Planning*. You can download these worksheets from our Web site (www.simplifiedstrategy.com). The figures in the book provide examples of how to fill the worksheets out. As you complete worksheets, you can assemble them in a loose-leaf notebook and have your own set to correspond with the information in this book.

Worksheet No.	Description	Figure No.	Text Page
1	**EXTERNAL SITUATION**		
1.1- n	Market Segment Analysis	4-3	47
1.2- n	Competitive Evaluations	5-1	52
1.3	Technology Assessment	5-2	57-58
1.4	Supplier Market Assessments	5-3	59
1.5	Current Economic Situation	5-4	62
1.6	Significant Regulations	5-5	63
2	**INTERNAL SITUATION**		
2.1	Balance Sheet	6-1	66
2.2	Five-Year Operating Statement	6-2	67
2.3	Measures of Success	6-5	72
2.4- n	Profitability Analysis	6-3	68
3	**CAPABILITIES AND COMPETENCIES**		
3.1	Capabilities Assessments	6-7	77-78
3.2	Strategic Competencies	7-2	86

Worksheet No.	Description	Figure No.	Text Page
4	**ASSUMPTIONS**		
4.1-n	Assumptions for Market Segments	9-1	106
4.2-n	Competition Assumptions for Market Segments	9-2	108
4.3	Other Important Assumptions	9-4	111
4.4	Perceived Opportunities	10-1	119
4.5-n	Opportunity Screening Worksheets	10-2	120-121
4.6	Perceived Threats	10-3	124
4.7	Industry Scenario	11-1	129
4.8	Winner's Profile	11-2	131
5	**STRATEGIES**		
5.1-n	Strategic Assessments	13-3	155
5.2	Strategic Issues	12-1	147-148
5.3	How Many Ways Could We Shoot Ourselves in the Foot?	14-1	174
5.4	Strategies	14-2	175-176
6	**GOALS AND OBJECTIVES**		
6.1	Mission Statement	15-2	182
6.2	Goals	15-3	184
6.3	Objectives	15-4	188
7	**ACTION PLANS**		
7.n	Action Plans	16-1, 16-2	194,198
8	**BUDGETS**		
8.1	Operating Budget	17-1	202
8.2	Investment Budget	17-3	205
8.3	Cash Flow Budget	17-2	203
8.4	Five Year Operating Statement	17-4	209
9	**SCHEDULES**		
9.1	Time Worksheet	17-5	212-213
9.2	Personal Annual Schedule	17-6	213
9.3	Planning Schedule	3-3	30
9.4	Monitoring Schedule	18-2	224

Index

personal annual schedules, 212–14, 216
Ph.D. phenomenon, 139
planning schedules, *30–31*
preferences, anticipating, 103
price
    avoiding competition on, 43
    competitive strategy based on, 161, 162–63
    as indicator of quality, 41
processes, and strategic competencies, 80
process flow, of simplified strategic planning, 28–29
process leaders, 19–20
process technology, 55
Procter & Gamble, 82
products and services strategic focus, 140–41, 145, *149*
product technology, 55
profitability analyses, 65, 68
profits
    analyzing, 65, 68
    versus cash flow, 70
    and the commodity/specialty market curve, 40
    as goal, 181–82
    making assumptions about, 104
proprietary position, 109
purchasing people, 54

Q
quality, and price, 41
quarterly tune-up meetings, 221, *223*

R
rating systems, for ideas, 117
raw materials strategic focus, 144, *149*
regulations, 61–63
research leaders, 46
resource planning
    for money, 200–207
    for time, 208–17

return on investment, 113
routine time, 210–14

S
safety regulations, 61
sales and distribution strategic focus, 144, *149*
scenario planning, 98
schedules
    for action plans, 216–17
    for routine time, 212–14
    for strategic planning, *30–31*
segmentation
    analyzing, 45–46
    approaches to, 42–44
    examples of, 44–45
    and future assumptions, 102–5
    worksheet for, 47
segmentation strategy, 162, 163
serendipity, 99–100
services strategic focus, 140–41, 149
service technology, 55
situation analysis, 28
skepticism, 17–18
skills, and strategic competencies, 80
Southwest Airlines, 37, 49, 180
Spartans, 74, 136
specialization. *See* focus
special projects time, 214–17
specialty markets
    versus commodity markets, 38–42
    competitive strategies for, 161–62
    dominating, 38
    indicators of, *41*
steam engines, 6
strategic assessment
    analyzing data, 156–60
    elements of, 150–53
    plotting data for, 154–56
strategic assessment matrix, 154–60
strategic competencies
    aligning focus with, 148–49
    elements of, 79–80

About the Authors

J. Peter Duncan. Before joining the Center for Simplified Strategic Planning, Peter Duncan held a wide variety of positions in several small technology based companies. In 1984, Peter was an original member of the start-up team that founded a semiconductor manufacturing operation specializing in custom circuits and contract manufacturing. Later, at another electronics manufacturer, Peter was part of a turn-around team that reestablished customer relationships and refocused the product strategy transforming the company into a customer driven, service organization with twice the output and a best in class cycle time.

Immediately prior to joining, the Center for Simplified Strategic Planning, Peter was the Director of Marketing for a mid-sized electronic components company. There he established the strategic direction for a new custom product line and profitably grew the business at over 80% per year during a four year period. With another product line, he identified changing market trends and repositioned the product line to attack a smaller segment where the company could dominate.

Peter's work at the Center for Simplified Strategic Planning has included assisting a wide range of companies from consumer product clients in furniture, hardware, local phone service, food products and household cleaning industries to industrial manufacturers of semiconductors, plastics, food processing equipment and packaging. His experience includes helping to develop strategic responses to rapidly changing market conditions for firms as diverse as software firms, government contractors, distributors and regulated interstate transportation companies.

Peter graduated from Middlebury College with a B.A. in Physics, and he holds a M.B.A. from the Amos Tuck School at Dartmouth College.

238

Robert W. Bradford. Starting as a software consultant in 1981, Robert Bradford worked at the forefront of information systems for six years before joining the Center for Simplified Strategic Planning. His past clients include a top supplier of management training services as well as two of the world's largest banks. One of Robert's earliest projects was a successful strategic management software product that continues to sell today. More recently, he headed up the operations planning department at a giant Japanese bank where he spearheaded the computerization of North American operations. Later, he moved to a major US money center bank where his innovations dramatically improved the bank's interest rate swap portfolio management techniques.

At the Center for Simplified Strategic Planning, Robert has successfully assisted many clients ranging from insurance companies to auto parts manufacturers and environmental services firms. Robert is the President of the Center for Simplified Strategic Planning and co-author of the *Simplified Strategic Planning Manual*. A graduate of Princeton University, with an A.B. in Military History, Robert holds an M.B.A. degree from the Amos Tuck School of Business Administration and has completed post-graduate work at the London Business School.

Brian Tarcy is a freelance writer and book developer living in Falmouth, Massachusetts. He is author or co-author of 12 books including *The Complete Idiot's Guide To Business Management* with Hap Klopp; *Tight Ships Don't Sink* with Gary Sutton; as well as collaborations with sports superstars Joe Theismann, Cam Neely, and Tom Glavine. He is currently a correspondent with *The Boston Globe* covering Cape Cod. He is a graduate of Ohio University in Athens, Ohio.